WRITING POEMS

BLOODAXE POETRY
HANDBOOKS: 2

Peter Sansom

WRITING
POEMS

BLOODAXE BOOKS

ISBN: 1 85224 204 3

First published 1994 by
Bloodaxe Books Ltd,
P.O. Box 1SN,
Newcastle upon Tyne NE99 1SN.

Bloodaxe Books Ltd acknowledges
the financial assistance of Northern Arts.

Cover printing by J. Thomson Colour Printers Ltd, Glasgow.

Printed in Great Britain by
Bell & Bain Limited, Glasgow, Scotland.

CONTENTS

'Art is the habit of the artist; and habits have to be rooted deep in the whole personality. They have to be cultivated like any other habit, over a long period of time, by experience; and teaching any kind of writing is largely a matter of helping the student develop the habit of art. I think this is more than just a discipline, although it is that; I think it is a way of looking at the created world and of using the senses so as to make them find as much meaning as possible in things.'

— FLANNERY O'CONNOR
Mystery and Manners

INTRODUCTION

This little book assumes you want to write as well as you can. It tries not to tell you what or how to write. Naturally I have my axe to grind and I hope you will be alert to the sound of sharpening in many of my convictions. You should be able to test the edge without having to put your head on the block.

In fact, I agree with those who think that no one can teach you how to write. 'Poetry must work out its own salvation in a man' as Keats says; 'it cannot be matured by law and precept, but by sensation and watchfulness in itself. That which is creative must create itself.' Keats's amazingly rapid development as a writer, though, is itself proof that people *can learn* to become better writers.

My main preoccupation in this book is with writing authentically. I mean by this *saying genuinely what you genuinely need to say.* I believe that when you write authentically the experience is the same as Keats's must have been when writing his great poems. It is true that, unless we have genius (and are living in a time congenial to it), we won't be writing as durably and eloquently as Keats; but we will have found what he called 'the true voice of feeling'. It is that voice which allows us to explore, order and make sense of our lives. That's the point of it, for me. The product of that experience may also be publishable – worth making public – but our poems are first of all for ourselves.

ONE

WRITING POEMS

Why write *poems*?

The American poet John Berryman said he wrote poems 'to get X into bed'. Philip Larkin was more English: 'I write to preserve something I've thought/felt/seen'. These reasons are not mutually exclusive and I suppose few people write entirely for one or other of them. Many write not so much to preserve as to find out what they've thought/felt/seen; most write, I imagine, not to impress others (wherever that may lead) but for self esteem and, in the best sense, to please themselves.

In practical terms I suppose people write poems because they enjoy using words and because they want to create something that didn't exist before. Writing poems is easier than, say, writing a novel, for which you need the time and creative stamina. Not to mention some notion of characterisation, plotting and so on. A poem can be written on a bus ride or at the end of a long day, and need not be technically demanding. But writing poetry is not simply a matter of convenience. Writing poetry is important to us, and personal, in a way that writing fiction, even the shortest of short stories, isn't. Perhaps the key word here is 'fiction'. We tend to feel that poems are *true*.

Gone

Heaven, at last, to feel the thump
of the hearse door shutting out the light
and to settle between my brothers;
one at each side. We move off

gently, through the low gears as if
I was a serious patient; as if my blood
couldn't stand the slightest jolt of speed.
I suppose the rain, damping, or the specks

of rain on the face of my watch
will be everlasting. Of this day.
And I wanted to do so well. To
hold on to every difficult breath

and keep that release for the pain
of everyday things: the children; clothes;
a space where she might have spoken;
anything. Because it comes. And suddenly.

Maybe tonight. Not the bed, empty, that's
one thing. But her watch, still ticking
and the loop of one, blonde hair
caught in her hairbrush. That's another.

This seems to me so accurately observed, so convincingly felt, it's hard to believe Simon Armitage hasn't actually suffered such a bereavement. Imaginatively, one might say, he has. Though at the time of writing, Armitage was twenty-four, unmarried and with, to the best of my knowledge, no children. It is the real detail in the poem, the real voice, I think, which makes it 'true'. Take that final image: 'her watch, still ticking / and the loop of one, blonde hair / caught in her hairbrush.' That kind of detail, in real life, would be heartbreaking; and so it is in poetry: unsentimental and written plainly, simply, just as it was seen. But it is *precise* too: 'the *loop* of one, blonde hair': we visualise that. For me, there is a slight but appreciable figurative meaning in there as well, since of course loops in a sense go on for ever, coming back on themselves: a notion he touches on earlier when he supposes those specks of rain on his watch are 'everlasting. Of this day.' Not that he tries to make much of the idea. It is just something, in that situation, the narrator thought about and expresses honestly, simply, vividly.

When we've written something that's true, almost all of us want to publish it.

Which brings us to...

Poetry and the marketplace

First of all let's get this straight. There is a popular notion that it's virtually impossible to get poetry published. I don't think so. Admittedly it is fairly difficult – but by no means impossible – to get *bad* poetry published. But if you are writing well – in whatever style – you will certainly find a publisher; though it may not be a publisher with nationwide distribution.

This is not to say that artistic merit ensures "success" in the poetry world. Many extremely gifted poets are neglected while lesser talents are fêted. Still, I take the view that good work will out.

The usual route to poetic "success" is by first getting known through appearing in magazines and perhaps winning a competition; then placing a small collection with a pamphlet-publisher; then having a book published. Note that this "success" often means an initial print run of no more than five hundred to a thousand copies, and that even if it is well reviewed your book is unlikely to sell out. Few poets make a living from book sales.

But of course publishing is essential. It gives a sense of yourself as a writer and affords some measure of feedback. It is, as I said, 'making public': but this does not necessarily mean having to get your poems in print. Show your work to friends, or, if you want to stay friends with your friends, join a writers' workshop. These are described in a later section. They are not for everyone, but everyone should try them at least once. Even so, publishing for most of us is really about getting your work in magazines and, ultimately, in a book.

Submitting poems to magazines

Conventional wisdom is that you should put a new poem in a drawer for six months before even thinking of sending it to a magazine. Few of us have the willpower. The new poem is almost always the best we've done and probably the best anyone's done this century. We need to show it to someone at once. The workshop is the best place for this because (a) you get an immediate response you can argue with; (b) you have the chance to read your poem objectively and change things that would get it rejected; and (c) you don't want to see your work in print and realise it's awful.

Primers such as this will tell you to 'study the market' and submit your manuscripts accordingly. So long as you are not *writing for* the market – though that is interesting as far as it goes (about as far as an exercise bike). I do think it's true that you should read the magazines you're sending to. They vary enormously in the kind of work they use, and you are asking for rejection if you are submitting blind. A few editors offer constructive criticism when they return mss, but from most you will get a printed slip. In any case, it is pointless publishing in places you don't respect. Do not doubt this: there are plenty of magazines that will publish tripe.

Some tripe-free magazine addresses are listed in Paul Hyland's *Getting Into Poetry*. For details of this and other useful publications such as *The Writer's Handbook*, see my bibliography.

The mechanics

• Send no more than six poems at a time – do you *have* six publishable poems?

• Are they all as good as work you've seen in that magazine?

• Always enclose a stamped addressed envelope.

• Type your work (preferably in black) on one side only of white A4 paper.

• Put your name and address on each sheet.

• Always keep a copy of each poem.

• Enclose a short covering letter, thanking the editor for her/his attention. By all means include *brief* biographical notes if you wish. They will not make a bad submission good, but they may capture the editor's attention.

• Some magazines reply within a week, others take *much* longer. If you haven't heard after a couple of months, a query (again enclosing s.a.e.) is not unreasonable. Your poems may have got lost in the post or down the back of the editorial settee.

If you can't beat them

Despite some evidence to the contrary, editors are human. And only human. They have their tastes and prejudices. Any fool can start a magazine – even a book press – and many do. You don't need a qualification. You need energy, enthusiasm, commitment. You need to be sanguine about the thousands writing poetry and none of them wanting to *read* it (how many poetry books have *you* bought this year?). Also you need some money. Not so much nowadays, in fact, with desk-top publishing and so on. If you have the desire to run a magazine or press, then do it. If you don't like what other magazines are producing, then set about publishing what you *do* like. Peter Finch's book, *How To Publish Your Poetry* will help [➡ *Bibliography*].

There is no final arbiter when it comes to how good a poem is. There is instead a consensus, usually among a small number of people (publishers, reviewers, literary organisations) which determine certain factors in a poet's standing.

Which is why, if you want to start a press, you should do. Geoff and Jeanette Hattersley's magazine, *The Wide Skirt*, has had a much bigger impact on the contemporary poetry scene than its modest format would suggest. It is typed, proof-read, pasted-up, printed (at a community printshop), collated, stapled together and mailed off to subscribers, all by the editors themselves. That is hard work but it keeps the costs to a minimum. Which is important. No one drives a Porsche in the small presses. Without *The Wide Skirt* and two or three other magazines and presses started around the same time, much of what seems to me the best contemporary poetry would not have found an outlet. What's more, certain poets would not have developed the way they have without the encouragement of the small presses and the example of their writers. Simon Armitage, whom I've just quoted, for instance. Deborah Randall too happens to have published in *The Wide Skirt*, which gives me leave to quote one of her poems and to go off on a little diversion:

Ballygrand Widow

So, you have gone my erstwhile glad boy,
whose body, I remember, stained my big cream bed,
and didn't we mix the day and the night in our play,
we never got up for a week.

If I must set my alarm again,
and feed the hungry hens in the yard,
and draw the milk from my cow on time,
and skulk my shame down Ballygrand Street
to get a drink,
it'll not be for you I think,
but my next husband,
a fine cock he shall be.

So, you are no more in this town
my lovely schoolboy, and how the floss
of your chin tickled me.
And you swam your hands all over,
you shouted for joy, the first time.
Ah, my darling!

I wear your mother's spit on my shoes,
the black crow priest has been to beat me.
But you gave me a belly full, the best,
and they shan't take it.
The days are unkind after you, they are empty.
I lie in the sheets, the very same sheets;
you smelled sweeter than meadow hay.
My beautiful boy you have killed me.

What I like about this is how the poem gets straight down to it; and how, for all its energy, it is actually controlled and artful, though never straying from the persona. That second line is really quite restrained, for example, if you consider the transferred epithet in the cream bed. The poem is concise: 'I wear your mother's spit on my shoes' tells us in one line what might take paragraphs in a novel. I get a sense of the whole person in this poem, the whole situation, the defiance and the loss, half celebration, half lament. 'The days are unkind after you, they are empty'; and that desolate last line. We don't doubt it is genuine speech, though it is clearly also poetry. Or perhaps you disagree. In a workshop once I heard 'Ballygrand Widow' described as 'smut that doesn't rhyme'. And for some, *if it doesn't rhyme, it's not a poem*.

'If it doesn't rhyme, it's not a poem'

If I had a penny for every time I'd heard this, I'd have three pound fifty by now. 'It's not a poem' is fighting talk. Rhymers are outraged by what 'modern poets' have done to poetry. My answer is: *I love rhyme*. What I'm not keen on is forced and predictable rhymes, rhymes that stop the poem saying what the writer really wants to say (sometimes saying its opposite), and everything in a jaunty metre, which doesn't suit the subject and every so often doesn't scan. Which is to say, not many people find it easy to rhyme well, but virtually anybody can rhyme badly. And if *anybody* could have written the poem, it simply won't be true to the person who wrote it.

In any case, the essence of all poetry has always been rhythm – not rhyme – and in many languages rhyme isn't used at all. English poetry didn't use rhyme until the time of Chaucer, when the fashion for rhyming verse was copied from French and Italian writers. Much of Shakespeare is written in blank verse, which of course doesn't rhyme. And though Robert Browning's 'Home Thoughts From Abroad' ('Oh, to be in England now that April's there') is one of our best known rhyming poems, a great deal of Browning's poetry doesn't rhyme. Wordsworth too. He rhymed his 'Daffodils', certainly, but he went for blank verse in his great epic poem *The Prelude*.

And look at Milton. Not only did he *not* rhyme *Paradise Lost*, but in its preface he was quite definite – in the 1660s – about this 'troublesome and modern bondage of rhyming'. He pointed out that 'rhyme was no necessary Adjunct or true Ornament of a Poem

13

or good Verse...' and went so far as to call it 'trivial' – 'the Invention of a barbarous Age, to set off wretched matter and lame Meeter'. And, which returns me to the business of being true to yourself, he noted also that rhyme was a constraint and hindrance which made poets express themselves differently 'and for the most part worse than else they would have expressed them.'

Of course, I don't like bad poems whatever they're dressed up in. But what I like even less than bad poems is the notion that there are hard and fast rules, that some things just aren't allowed.

We talk about poetry as if there was only one of it. In a review in *Iron* magazine, Bill Turner remarked that poems are like fruit. They come in all shapes, sizes, textures and colours and certain kinds will never be to one's taste. It seems to me some readers are like the young lad just after the war, not thinking much to his first banana because he didn't know to peel it. Some poems are tomatoes and for some readers a tomato will always be a vegetable. This next one for instance. But if you listen you can hear those irregular rhythms *are* working, and the witty rhymes and half-rhymes seem to me irresistible – even if it is shaped like a runner-bean.

Ode

'To depict a [bicycle], you must first come to love [it].'
ALEXANDER BLOK

I swear by every rule in the bicycle
owner's manual

that I love you, I, who have repeatedly,
painstakingly,

with accompanying declaration of despair,
tried to repair

you, to patch things up,
to maintain a workable relationship.

I have spent sleepless nights
in pondering your parts – those private

and those that all who walk the street
may look at –

wondering what makes you tick
over smoothly, or squeak.

O my trusty steed,
my rusty three-speed,

I would feed you the best oats
if oats

were applicable.
Only linseed oil

will do
to nourish you.

I want
so much to paint

you,
midnight blue

mudgutter black
and standing as you do, ironic

at the rail
provided by the Council –

beautiful
the sun caught in your back wheel –

or at home in the hall, remarkable
among other bicycles,

your handlebars erect.
Allow me to depict

you thus. And though I can't do justice
to your true opinion of the surface

of the road –
put into words

the nice distinctions that you make
among the different sorts of tarmac –

still I'd like to set the record of our travels straight.
I'd like you to know that

not with three-in-one
but with my own

heart's
spittle I anoint your moving parts.

GILLIAN ALLNUTT

As it happens, it seems to me harder just now to write good free verse than it was even a decade ago. Perhaps that is partly why *form is back!* And about time too. Writers overlook a useful tool when they discard form and especially rhyme.

In any case the fact is that a great deal of contemporary poetry *does* rhyme. It does not always have a thumping rhythm, which is what people tend to mean by 'rhyme', and it doesn't always have the kind of effects we find in, for example, Keats. Which is in some ways a shame. And prompts the obvious question:

Why not write like Keats?

Keats is the genuine article; his poems and letters (jammed with insights into poetry and life) are essential reading. He lived, briefly, in the early nineteenth century. At twenty-one he wrote 'On First Looking Into Chapman's Homer':

Much have I travell'd in the realms of gold,
    And many goodly states and kingdoms seen;
    Round many western islands have I been
Which bards in fealty to Apollo hold.
Oft of one wide expanse had I been told
    That deep-brow'd Homer ruled as his demesne;
    Yet did I never breathe its pure serene
Till I heard Chapman speak out loud and bold:
Then felt I like some watcher of the skies
    When a new planet swims into his ken;
Or like stout Cortez when with eagle eyes
    He star'd at the Pacific – and all his men
Look'd at each other with a wild surmise –
    Silent, upon a peak in Darien.

This is a pretty good sonnet by anybody's standards. Particularly the sestet (last six lines), which is astonishing now but in 1818 I imagine shook people up. No one had written quite like that before. The octave is not bad either, and notice all those inversions: 'Which bards in fealty to Apollo hold'. To fit the metre and effect the rhyme with 'gold', Keats alters the natural word-order ('Which bards hold in fealty...'); likewise in the next line ('had I been told'). And all those undeniably "poetic" words: 'bards', 'fealty', 'demesne'. Well, if this was good enough for arguably our greatest poet after Shakespeare, why not follow his example?

The first consideration is that unless you are Keats, some of these devices are difficult to pull off. Altering the word order puts an "unnatural" word to the end of the line, and, since the end-word carries extra emphasis – because we pause there – it had better be able to bear that stress. We might quibble with that rather limp-looking 'had I been told', for instance, until we realise that Keats needs to emphasise 'told': the poem is about discovering something for himself which he had only heard talked about before.

This poem will not date. Keats's 'true voice of feeling', the honesty, fluency and depth of his imagination, these are timeless. The way it is expressed, though, is tied to the time he wrote. The syntax and diction which place the poem in Keats's time equally take it out of ours. We write differently now. In one sense it's a matter of fashion (just as we wear different clothes now); in another it's necessity. Keats's age "needed" poems the way he wrote them. If he'd written in the manner of, say, Alexander Pope, he could not have said what he did. He could not have found the 'true voice of feeling'. The literary trend at that time was in reaction against Pope and the whole Augustan mode of writing. The muse on a rocking horse, Keats called it, in fact. Similarly, if Keats had somehow managed to write like, say, Ted Hughes, his audience would have been flummoxed. It would have been no use to them. Even as it was, Keats died long before a large appreciative audience was found for his poetry. (Some of the reviews he saw of his first book were devastating.) Because he was doing something new, he was not understood. Wordsworth – who seems never to have bothered reading Keats (they did meet; Keats found him condescending) – came up with this dictum in a letter to a friend: 'Every great writer in accordance as he is great, must form the taste by which he will be appreciated.' I am not sure this is *always* the case, nor that a writer need do it – can do it – on his or her own, but it is worth thinking about.

Which brings me back, at last, to the business of the small presses, and why more people should start them, write for them, read them, support them. T.S. Eliot published in little magazines – indeed he edited one for a while – and Faber and Faber have not always been an institution. Bloodaxe Books began as a one-man operation performed on a kitchen table. *The Wide Skirt* started small and, like many other such outfits, *prefers* to stay small. That does not mean it is not influential or for want of a better word important. Which is to say, we should not judge a book by its staples.

Discrimination

Well, none of this need concern you. Your job is writing poems. Like editing, though, writing poems means learning discrimination, finding out what you like and don't like regardless of what anybody else thinks. The more you read poems and talk with others about them, and the more criticism you learn from, the more discriminating a reader you will become. This is not as daunting or boring as it sounds. And anyway it is unavoidable. You have to make yourself your own best critic. So that when editors return your work you can decide if they're right or don't know their poetic arse from their elbow.

One other thing. Editors do not want to reject your poems. There's nothing they'd like more than to find them brilliant and publish you to the glory of their magazine.

More discrimination

'All poetry is obscure to the closed intelligence,' the writer John Wain has said. It is not the individual he is attacking, though, but the situation of poetry:

At the moment, it seems to be accepted as a matter of course that there is no possible means of understanding poetry; as I write, the experts are disagreeing as to whether Dylan Thomas was a good poet or not, and the "reading public" are simply watching the battle with their heads swivelling as at a tennis match; it is just taken for granted that there is no hope of seeing for oneself, of checking the opinions of the experts against one's own reactions to the poems...No, poetry is an impenetrable mystery. And not only "modern" poetry, which is supposed to be "obscure". The man who complains of the obscurity of modern poetry does so, usually, because the contemporary is the only kind that lies in his path; he would find all poetry difficult, if he ever looked at it, but he does not open his weekly paper and find a few lines of Shakespeare or Dante to shake his head over. Imagine his reaction to Wordsworth's 'Lucy' poems! – recall in fact what *was*, as a matter of literary history, the reaction to them!

This was written in 1955 in the introduction to a book Wain hoped might 'get people to be less frightened of literary criticism; to show them, if possible, that they can scale even very high poems without being roped together and led by a guide'. We have come a long way since then: we have fewer weekly papers and almost none that publish poems. And where is that 'reading public' today? Not with their noses in lit crit, that's for sure, and blissfully unaware that that Thomas tennis match is now well into its millionth set. Wain might have predicted it, his point being just that no one takes any notice of the critics, who 'get better and better, but are only writing for one another; none of that intelligence is flowing into the common stock – as one sees from a glance at what actually gets published, praised, taken seriously, given literary awards and so on...'

What is irksome about all this, and one of the reasons I quote it at length, is the sense Wain has of so much Us and Them. I wonder if things are changing. Let's imagine – since you and I have powerful imaginations – that it is. And so, with a lighter heart, go on with

Yet more discrimination

There are many examples of poets who have not been properly valued till after their death, but the obvious career move has drawbacks. And it doesn't matter how many feet under you are if your work is bad. Which is why you have to learn discrimination: no one can do this for you, finally; no one else knows exactly what you are trying to do. In the end you have to be able to judge for yourself how well you are writing. And, often, how badly. The most important equipment for a writer of course, according to Nobel Prizewinner Ernest Hemingway, is 'a built-in, shock-proof shit detector'.

Do not trust to posterity. Even hindsight is not twenty-twenty, and the notion of poetry being 'winnowed by time' is unstable. Until Eliot (and others) revived his reputation, John Donne languished in relative obscurity. Certain of his qualities appealed to the sensibility of Eliot's time, and Donne, through essays and books on him and subsequently by becoming a set-text on academic courses, regained his place in the canon.

I.A. Richards has pointed out that several 'classics' are more admired than read; that just *because* a poem has been reprinted over the decades, people *assume* it is good. He cites for instance 'Hiawatha'. Poems that spoke for one age may be dumb for another. This is not to say that, like Donne's, they cannot find their voice again. Nor should we forget that some ages may be better readers of poetry than others. And that each age is made up of individual readers. 'On First Looking Into Chapman's Homer' is not the same poem for you as it is for me. It was even more different a poem for Keats and his contemporaries. Each poem is utterly unique to the individual reader, and what's more it changes as the reader changes.

So, we may say, since it is all ultimately subjective,* we need not trouble our heads about whether a poem is good or not. Quite the reverse. If we don't appraise poems ourselves, then we leave it entirely to others, not least the current literati. Also, it would mean incidentally that to you Shakespeare is of no greater literary value than a *Dallas* scriptwriter.†

There are no absolute standards; but that is not the same as saying there is no bad writing. Maybe we can't judge which is, aesthetically, the finer of two Chippendale chairs. But we may feel sure that either of those Chippendales is a sight finer than the chair you bought at MFI. Especially if you can only get three of the legs on. After which cheap joke, I should say that though an MFI chair may be worth less than a Chippendale, it might well be more comfortable. Then you have to ask yourself what you want it for, of course.

Randall Jarrell said that (as a reviewer) he was often sent work which, though sincere, was like getting ripped-out arms and legs through the post with 'this is a poem' scrawled on in lipstick. Here is the plain fact of it. There are literally thousands of bad poems sent to editors every week, many by people who have devoted themselves to their writing over several years; most by people convinced their writing is not only original but almost literally crying out to be published. The bulk of it, frankly, is dreadful. I will discuss the more common failings later, but various though they are, bad poems are the same in one essential: they are not true. They do not genuinely say what they genuinely need to say.

---

* 'Values grow out of the historical process of valuation, which they in turn help us to understand. The answer to historical relativism is not a doctrinaire absolutism which appeals to unchanging human nature or the universality of art. We must be able to refer a work of art to the values of its own time and of all the periods subsequent to its own. A work of art is both "eternal" (i.e. preserves a certain identity) and "historical" (i.e. passes through a process of traceable development).' – Wellek and Warren: *Theory of Literature*.

† Which is not an untenable position of course. In any case, everyone is entitled to their opinion. Some opinions are better informed than others, we might say; but informed by what? I can think of writers who would take issue with my cultural assumptions and indeed those which underlie the whole canon of English Literature.

Reading

'The first skill of any writer is the skill to read,' says Michael Schmidt, poet, critic and managing director of Carcanet Press. Reading poetry is a skill that many – even published – writers never acquire. Of all the variables that come into play here, the quality of your reading above all informs the quality of your writing. (And it's often been noted that if everyone who wrote poetry bought poetry books there would be a publishing boom; then supply-and-demand would mean that you'd have more chance of being published.)

As it is, many beginning poets will say they haven't time to read poems as well as write them. Well, OK, but then you are wasting the little time you do have. You are writing in the dark if you read no one but yourself. And in the dark you can't even read yourself properly.

So let's take it that, if you're not already a reader of contemporary poetry, you're convinced by now you should be. The trouble is knowing *which* poets. There are simply too many slim volumes and not all of them slim. A section of this book is devoted to writers I think will help you; it should prove that not all contemporary poetry is tedious and incomprehensible. Some of it assuredly is. The greater part of it, though, is accessible and very entertaining – some might say rather too much so, but that's a can of worms we'll keep the lid on for the moment. Instead let's get straight in to:

Clever order of ideas, chapter.

Buckets

There are as many ways of writing a poem as there are writers. And almost as many theories about what the writing process involves. Personally, I subscribe to the well theory. You drop a bucket down into the subconscious and reel up the poem. What comes up depends what's down there, of course, and it may not all come up at once. But it mostly depends I think on your bucket. The bucket, you may have guessed, is language. Some buckets haven't enough capacity while others are too big and the lip remains above the water; some take an ambitious load and the line snaps. There are even poets who get drawn into the well and are stuck there shouting incomprehensibly up to a little circle of the real world far above their heads (though they think it is beneath them). More often, a novice may be using a worn out bucket, handed down from the 19th century, full of holes, more of a colander.

To continue with this <u>ludicrous metaphor</u> just a little longer: the more varied and flexible your language and technique, the greater the chance your bucket will be right for you and up to the job.

Forget buckets. Look at it this way. Not all imaginative experience – not all creative raw material – is the same; but you will write as though it were if, for instance, you can only write limericks. Then your imagination will veto certain subjects: it is hard to craft a moving elegy beginning 'There once was my father who died'.

The tabula rasa theory, reading and garlic

'Ah but,' some will persist, 'I want to write as no one else has ever written, so I mustn't read anyone for fear of contaminating my bucket.' This is the tabula rasa or empty-headed approach. Nice, but it will not hold water. Even the most illiterate of us has already been influenced. To write you need words. You learned them some-where and you learned contexts along with them. *To write a poem* you need words plus some organising principle to make it a poem and not just a jumble. You learned that somewhere too. At school you may have been spared poetry, but have you steered clear of hymns, pop music, advertising jingles, greetings cards?

It's possible that, with the bare minimum, you can eke out a style. A cursory reading of a major talent will give you something to work with. T.S. Eliot or Sylvia Plath, for instance, get into your blood like garlic. And it's powerful stuff. You won't know why your friends are keeling over but sooner or later someone will tell you you reek.

You need to read deeply and widely. Reading is appropriating technique and procedures, not just picking up verbal tics. If you arrest the process of influence there, you will be like the flamingo, pink because your diet is all prawns. You need to be ranging among literature and giving yourself up to poems. Submitting to them. And, above all, reading them *aloud*. Learning poems by heart is often enlightening: you really get at a poem that way, and you realise there are parts of it you'd been misreading or had skated over altogether.

Close-reading may – but does not always – mean you will go through phases: the Dylan Thomas phase perhaps followed by the Philip Larkin, then maybe the Robert Lowell. You will not be writ-ing well; you will be ventriloquising. There are many published writers who never get further than this stage. They spend their lives talking from someone else's mouth. And actually some people like listening to these poets best, because it makes no demands – it is easy to hear what you've heard before. But your search should be for writers and combinations of writers who will not so much form as *release* your own voice (or voices).

For this to happen, you will need to be reading intelligently. Not studying for exams with a pencil poised to deface the margin, but not dreamily either or you'll wake at the bottom of the page no wiser. A poem is only as good as its reader. If you approach a poem expecting it to be dull the chances are it will be; you will be blind to its virtues and deaf to what it could tell you. When it comes to poetry, everyone's a critic. Not me and you, though. We're reading as poets, as fellow practioners. We may sometimes be looking to learn new perspectives and devices. But first of all we are reading poems because we like reading poems. We like being open and alert to what the poem is doing.

We want to enjoy the poem fully, and this will require several readings – but sometimes we just feel like ploughing through a book of poems and only mulling over two or three that catch our attention. That's no problem. We're drawn back, I think, to good poems; and we read them in different ways at different times. Many writing skills will come to us unconsciously from our reading (and more will come as we become more practised readers); but we can also be on the look out for them: we may note for instance the way a particular poem – like 'Traveling through the Dark', which I discuss in the next chapter – balances half-rhyme and internal rhyme, and we can consider how to use that technique ourselves. Most often, though, we don't know that we've learned a skill until we practice it in one of our poems.

However we come by them, it is *crucial* that we make those skills our own: otherwise our poems – full of the requisite metre, imagery, assonance, alliteration and so on – will be little more than applications for the job of poet. Our poems have to be in tenure. Our poems, I am tempted to say rather rhetorically, have to be *us*. However we have learned from other writers, and however heightened and ordered the language – our poems have to be spoken in our own voice, and (even if, like Deborah Randall in 'Ballygrand Widow', we are using a persona) they have to be true to our own experience.

Well, this is all very high-sounding, but it's also very general and it doesn't tell you how to write poems. Which is as it should be. Learn from other people, yes. But when you come to write a poem, you do that yourself and you do it regardless of how you think you *ought* to write. Please remember this, when I'm being prescriptive in the rest of this book. I think there are things you might well avoid doing, and practices which may well help you to write more authentically. But while the poem is getting written you have to trust it and yourself and do the best you can with what's to hand. The more reading you've done, and the more thought you've put in, the more serviceable your bucket will be.

A POEM ANALYSED

'Traveling through the Dark': a poem analysed

I want briefly to flesh out the things I've been saying. So I'll look in some detail at what might be thought of as a model poem. It is much anthologised and I expect it is often used in seminars. Some poems you love, but what can you say about them? Others are chock full of all the poetic devices students need to know in order to pass exams – and not unnaturally it is these poems which find their way most easily into the canon of English Literature. 'Traveling through the Dark', by William Stafford, seems to me very fine, and certainly worth an hour of any class's time. It is so well made, so – almost tenderly – achieved, that in its modest, meditative way, it is able to broach huge areas of human experience. Discussing the poem, a group invariably turns to discussing the issues raised by it, though it is by no means explicit in declaring those issues.

I like Stafford's poem very much. But I'll admit from the start here that it seems to me factitious. Which is to say it is rather too conscious of its aims. Or as the dictionary says: 'Made for a special purpose; not genuine; not natural; artificial.' A factitious poem in my terms is – you may have guessed – simply *not true*. I may be (and in a way I hope I am) doing Stafford a great injustice. It is the title poem of a collection which won a National Book Award. My feeling that it is factitious certainly damages but does not invalidate the poem for me; and as you will see from how much I've got to say about it, it does anything but diminish my admiration for Stafford as a craftsman. Nor does that phrase of Wordsworth's about murdering to dissect apply, I think. The more we look at Stafford's poem, the better it becomes – or rather, the better we become as readers of it.

You'll gather from the spelling that Stafford is American.

Traveling through the Dark

Traveling through the dark I found a deer
dead on the edge of the Wilson River road.
It is usually best to roll them into the canyon:
that road is narrow; to swerve might make more dead.

By glow of the tail-light I stumbled back of the car
and stood by the heap, a doe, a recent killing;
she had stiffened already, almost cold.
I dragged her off; she was large in the belly.

My fingers touching her side brought me the reason –
her side was warm; her fawn lay there waiting,
alive, still, never to be born.
Beside that mountain road I hesitated.

The car aimed its lowered parking lights;
under the hood purred the steady engine.
I stood in the glare of the warm exhaust turning red;
around our group I could hear the wilderness listen.

I thought hard for us all – my only swerving –
then pushed her over the edge into the river.

Let's start with the title, which is oblique, intriguing. It has a literal meaning first; the poem might equally have been called 'Driving
at Night'. Except Stafford is pointing that it is not the driving
that is important but the travelling; not the night but the darkness. We are expected to pick up the metaphorical import in the
real incident. Without resorting to crude allegory, he is clearly
intending us to consider in it something of "life's journey". And it
is a journey not taken after dark, but *through* it. Two meanings
here then: we travel uncertainly, sometimes, in darkness; and it is
through such experiences that we, as individuals, *progress*.

The poem will not be reduced to a specific figurative meaning
but, in 'Beside that mountain road I hesitated' and again in the
final couplet, it is made clear that the whole piece is detailing and
enacting someone's struggle with a moral dilemma, while 'the
wilderness' waits for the outcome. A man pulls over on a narrow
road because a killed deer is in the way. He finds it is pregnant
and its fawn still alive. He must decide whether to drive round it
and continue his journey (which may 'make more dead') or take
the responsibility of killing the fawn to clear the route. That is the
'traveling'. As a matter of fact, from the moment the poem – the
car – is stopped by the obstacle in the first line, it does no literal
travelling. At the end of the poem the car does not start up again.
The only thing that goes anywhere, apart from the man 'stumbling',
is the deer as it gets dragged about and is finally rolled off out of
the last line.

At which point the class wants to become a seminar on abortion, green issues, pacificism. In an unguarded moment I once mentioned to a group that Stafford was a conscientious objector in the Second World War. Well, that's it, then: the sincerity of the poem is underwritten. Returning to the poem qua poem gets us no further than admiring the archetypes: what does that 'river' *mean* – the flow of time? of life? Water – the utterly clear, utterly pure, staple of all life – comes down off that mentioned 'mountain', joins the river and makes for the sea, where it is taken up in the cycle of regeneration, renewal. And isn't there some classical river...?

We distrust poems that have palpable designs on us, as Keats would say; and we do so even when those designs are not explicit. My problems with 'Traveling through the Dark' start just there. It seems to me it is all designs, not vulnerable to interpretations but with them *built in* for no other reason than that they be teased out. It is not an 'application for the job of poet' but an essay question 'discuss with reference to'.

Poems are sometimes likened to magic. Some poems are magic. We can explain how they work, even perhaps why they work, but the process of writing remains a mystery. Others are sleight of hand. They seem magic until we know how it was done, until we realise it is a trick. Aren't all poems "tricks"? Poems are verbal constructs. They use devices, procedures, some of which the poet may be conscious of as s/he writes. My feeling is that the most authentic writing comes of working with more than "conscious" thought, when the process is organic, when it relies upon – in Coleridge's phrase – the 'shaping spirit of imagination'. This is still using devices, but using them instinctively and prompted by the language, the patterns a poem naturally wants to follow and develop. It's very possible that Stafford worked this way, of course, but I remain unconvinced. And to be sure, everyone is capable of instinctively using devices in a hamfisted way or of unconsciously choosing the wrong devices. Not Stafford, by any means. He is sincere and he is very good indeed. Let's look at some of the devices he employs.

The poem comprises four quatrains* and a final couplet. There is no run on between the stanzas, and all but two of the lines are themselves units of sense. This allows the poem to release its narrative and commentary cleanly and concisely. It also gives the feel-

---

* The jargon I have fallen into is explained, if you need it, in the glossary.

ing that the poem is considered, the ideas neatly boxed or parcelled up. The two enjambements ('I found a deer / dead...' and 'I stumbled back of the car / and stood...') have a clear but unforced dramatic effect.

Unobtrusive near-rhymes in the second and fourth lines of each stanza hold the poem together: road/dead; killing/belly; waiting/hesitated; engine/listen. And then the final couplet, whose near-rhyme is all the more attractive for being delicate, understated. It relies, this last couplet (as, with the exception of the first stanza, the rest do) on the rhythmical echo of feminine endings and alliteration (here the Vs, and notice also how near 'river' is to 'listen', effecting, with that extra interlaced rhyme, a satisfying close).

The rhymes serve a semantic purpose too (it's worth remembering how many poems use rhyme merely as binding). Each rhyme is drawn from an allied or contiguous word. I mean that the rhyme words relate to each other in meaning as well as in sound. For instance, it is the 'road' that will make more 'dead'; the 'killing' is of something which has life in its 'belly'; the fawn is 'waiting' while the man is 'hesitating'; the car, itself inanimate, man-made, is alive: we hear the purr of its 'steady engine' as does the wilderness, which must 'listen'; the man's decision is his 'only swerving' and it is this that dumps the doe in the 'river' (and therefore into all the metaphorical paraphernalia I mentioned that the river carries).

There is alliteration. The Ds for instance in the opening two lines, and – particularly apt – in 'under the hood purred the steady engine' (where in tandem with the Ts they come in at exact – mechanical – intervals). The Ms in the last line of the first stanza are more difficult to explain, but I expect it could be done. There is assonance, in the rhyme words and in such as 'her side was warm; her fawn' (which is especially accomplished since it strengthens the balance of idea and rhythm either side of that semi-colon).

The triumph, for me, is the internal rhyme, which shores the poem up and pulls the reader on. Accoustic effects work on us all the more profoundly because we do not have to search them out. In these above all Stafford's poem strikes me as consummate and completely unshowy in its craftsmanship. The near-rhymed end-words may look rather loose – even, some people might think, a bit lazy; but they do not *sound* loose. And this is because in each stanza there is a three-line internal rhyme pattern which threads through to a key end-word. As: lines 2-4: dead/best/dead; in 5-7: glow/doe/cold; 9-11: brought/fawn/born; 13-15: ahead/steady/red.

'Traveling through the Dark' is a gift for practical criticism. Just as the near-rhyme is deceptively casual, the rhythmical pulse in the poem can be shown to be more artful than it at first appears. Inexperienced students come a cropper in that they can identify pentameter but then struggle to find the iambs. Smiling benignly from on high, the tutor is able to begin a discussion of metrical schemes, and to introduce the notions of distributed stress and hypermetrical and catalectic feet. Prosody is all Greek to most people, and the scientific-sounding jargon is forbidding, especially if you assume poems have been put together like a computer program. Poems do not conform to given metre, they are based on and make use of metre. Here are two of the most famous lines of iambic pentameter in the language:

The curfew tolls the knell of passing day

To be or not to be that is the question

The first is regular:

$$\underset{\text{The cur}}{-\ /}\ |\ \underset{\text{few tolls}}{-\ /}\ |\ \underset{\text{the knell}}{-\ /}\ |\ \underset{\text{of pass}}{-\ /}\ |\ \underset{\text{ing day}}{-\ /}$$

Five (pent) iambic (unstressed/stressed) feet. The second example can be read as hypermetric (having an extra, unstressed syllable) but otherwise regular:

$$\underset{\text{To be}}{-\ /}\ |\ \underset{\text{or not}}{-\ /}\ |\ \underset{\text{to be}}{-\ /}\ |\ \underset{\text{that is}}{-\ /}\ |\ \underset{\text{the ques}}{-\ /}\ |\ \underset{\text{tion}}{(-)}$$

But you would have to be a very good or else an am-dram actor to have the stress falling on 'is' instead of (which the sense seems to require) 'that'.

In the Gray poem we hear a bell tolling, regular as clockwork. In Shakespeare's verse we hear a man thinking something through to himself.*

'Traveling through the Dark' is basically a five stress line. The underlying metre is iambic – though the opening stanza, which I'm going to look at here, is I think largely trochaic (stressed, unstressed); and it is by no means regular. Faced with scanning the poem, some students complain that there is no pattern and indeed that line 3 falls to prose. I think you can argue that lines two and four balance exactly and in fact that the stresses in line

---

* Metre is discussed in Chapter Seven.

three, though unexpected, are very well suited to its sense: those unusual amphibrachs 'to roll them' and 'the canyon' have the force of rhyme and bundle the line across that hesitating, cliff's-edge pause of the trochee.

Traveling | through the | dark I | found a | deer

dead on the | edge of the | Wilson | River | road.

It is u | sually best | to roll them | into | the canyon:

that road is | narrow; to | swerve might | make more | dead. (−)

Line one I take to be trochaic pentameter with a catalectic foot. The line break and change of metre in the second line *wrong*-foots us: we are shocked to find the deer dead. I read that line as two dactyls which pause (like the meaning) before settling back into trochees beyond the 'Wilson River road'. It could be scanned otherwise, I know, but the internal rhyme ('dead on the | edge of the') suggests dactyls, and the previous line's trochees. The third line I hear as two anapaests, and two amphibrachs balanced round a trochee. The fourth line repeats the metre of the second, even to its possible alternative scansion; though I stay with this scansion because the line also repeats the assonance: 'dead on the | edge of the' and 'that road is | narrow to'. The metrical echo is satisfying aesthetically, but it also furthers the poem's underlying argument: in stressing 'that road' we are alerted to a symbolical meaning. Other roads may be wider, easier; but *that* road is narrow, difficult, fraught with danger.

Scanning lines like these is also fraught with danger. It is possible to scan them, with equal justice, entirely differently. Nevertheless, the rest of the poem is amenable to similar metrical discussion, and yields similar patternings, though we might argue about how they shape up. What I think we would agree on is that though at first sight 'Traveling through the Dark' looks casual, its rhythms are intimately (though complexly) married to the sense they carry.

We might have guessed as much from the many syntactical inversions: 'to swerve might make more dead'; 'By glow of the tail light I stumbled back of the car'; 'My fingers touching her side brought me the reason'; 'Beside that mountain road I hesitated'; 'under the hood purred the steady engine'; 'around our group I could hear the wilderness listen'. Only the first of these and the fifth 'under the hood...' seem to me to depart from standard usage, though they all have a poetic job to do.

*

Discussing the poem is of course more difficult and contentious than appreciating it. And what's more, there's always the danger of using a poem merely to exercise your critical ingenuity. Which is to say that, though considering poems in detail – working out *why* you like them – is obviously worthwhile, it is important first and foremost simply to experience the poem. For me, that generally means finding a quiet place where I can read it aloud.

And after all of this, I have to say I'm still not sure how far Stafford has *deliberately* not mentioned the obvious choice in 'Traveling through the Dark': that of slitting the deer open to try and save its fawn.

THREE

THE SPIRIT OF THE AGE

The pendulum in literary history

I mentioned a return to formal poetry. This can be explained to some extent by 'the pendulum theory of literary history' – the way one "movement" reacts against the one that immediately precedes it. New writers often gather energy and impetus from being radical, from doing something the last lot didn't. I think it's human nature. Do what – or if you daren't, then at least *wear* what – will most get up your parents' noses.

It may have something to do with art as *defamiliarisation*.

The Russian Formalist Victor Schlovsky maintained that the end and justification of all art is that it defamiliarises things which have become dulled and even invisible to us through habit, and thus enables us to perceive the world afresh.

...What is foregrounded by one generation of writers becomes background for the next. Thus, Eliot and Pound foregrounded their poetry, with its bewildering shifts of registers, dislocations of syntax and esoteric allusion, against the background of the orthodox poetic taste of the early twentieth century. The 1930s poets in turn foregrounded their poetry against the background of the Eliot-Pound modernist mode by adopting a more consistent tone of voice, deviating very little from orthodox syntax and filling their poems with ample reference to the facts of contemporary life.

...And so on up to the present day.

[David Lodge: *Working with Structuralism*]

Since we've just been through a period when anything went, the most radical thing is to be conservative. One of the oldest forms, the sonnet, for example, has suddenly just now been taken up in earnest and everywhere at once. The interesting thing is that when you write a sonnet you in some sense continue the tradition (readers will bring their knowledge of other sonnets) while doing what you can in that form. Some work with the form, others against it. On 3 May 1819, John Keats said in a letter 'I have been endeavouring to discover a better sonnet stanza than we have. The legitimate does not suit the language over-well from the pouncing rhymes – the other kind appears too elegiac – and the couplet at the end of it has seldom a pleasing effect – I do not pretend to have succeeded – it will explain itself.' Which it does, though I can't resist explaining – since nowadays we're less used to classical references – that the sandals (the interweaving rhymes and run-on lines) belong to Perseus. They are winged sandals he wore when rescuing the beautiful Andromeda from a rock she'd been chained to in the sea.

'If by dull rhymes'

If by dull rhymes our English must be chain'd,
And, like Andromeda, the Sonnet sweet
Fetter'd, in spite of pained loveliness,
Let us find out, if we must be constrain'd,
Sandals more interwoven and complete
To fit the naked foot of Poesy:
Let us inspect the Lyre, and weigh the stress
Of every chord, and see what may be gain'd
By ear industrious, and attention meet;
Misers of sound and syllable, no less
Than Midas of his coinage, let us be
Jealous of dead leaves in the bay wreath crown;
So, if we may not let the Muse be free,
She will be bound with garlands of her own.

'Attention meet' (fitting): that's the thing. Inspecting the lyre, weighing the stress of every chord, is working *with* as much as *adapting* the form.

And now, one more poem, mainly because it is a favourite of mine, but partly to show that "form" needn't mean iambic pentameter and end-rhyme. Form is 'expectation satisfied' as Randall Jarrell says Kenneth Burke says. It was written in 1935 by Basil Bunting, a writer whose ear was certainly 'industrious' and who was always 'miserly of sound and syllable':

33

The Orotava Road

Four white heifers with sprawling hooves
           trundle the waggon.
    Its ill-roped crates heavy with fruit sway.
The chisel point of the goad, blue and white,
           glitters ahead,
    a flame to follow lance-high in a man's hand
who does not shave. His linen trousers
           like him want washing.
    You can see his baked skin through his shirt.
He has no shoes and his hat has a hole in it.
           'Hu! vaca! Hu! vaca!'
    he says staccato without raising his voice;
'Adios caballero' legato but
           in the same tone.
    Camelmen high on muzzled mounts
boots rattling against the panels
           of an empty
    packsaddle do not answer strangers.
Each with his train of seven or eight tied
           head to tail they
    pass silent but for the heavy bells
and plip of slobber dripping from
           muzzle to dust;
    save that on sand their soles squeak slightly.
Milkmaids, friendly girls between
           fourteen and twenty
    or younger, bolt upright on small
trotting donkeys that bray (they arch their
           tails a few inches
    from the root, stretch neck and jaw forward
to make the windpipe a trumpet)
           chatter. Jolted
    cans clatter. The girls' smiles repeat
the black silk curve of the wimple
           under the chin.
    Their hats are absurd doll's hats
or flat-crowned to take a load.
           All have fine eyes.
    You can guess their balanced nakedness
under the cotton gown and thin shift.

They sing and laugh.
They say 'Adios!' shyly but look back
more than once, knowing our thoughts
and sharing our
desires and lack of faith in desire.

The spirit of the age

I should point out that literary fashions – like all fashions – are part and parcel of the times in which they occur. They express (and to an extent define) what Hazlitt called 'the spirit of the age'. Wordsworth and Coleridge – and indeed Hazlitt – were very much aware, for instance, of the French Revolution. The Industrial revolution too, for that matter, had a decisive influence on literary history. In our time, we might consider how far the invention of television has affected reading and writing habits. There are smaller reactions too, constantly, linked to what is happening in society. 'Pop' poetry was intimately related to fashion in its broad sense. And there seems to be for instance a correlation between hem-length and economics: the mini-skirt was so to speak at its height during the prosperous 60s, that general feeling of well-being and optimism which disappeared around the time England failed to retain the World Cup.

All of which brings us to you, writing now. If you are using 19th century language and its attendant literary conventions – if you are writing like Keats – then you are likely ipso facto to be writing 19th century pastiche: you are trying to express a modern sensibility through another age's words and frames of reference. Writing in this way seems to me like those pubs that install plastic "oak" beams and fittings: yearning, in a wholly false way, for something which is past and, if recoverable at all, can never be achieved by simply getting job-lots of archaic "poetry" words and phrases. You know the sort of thing: *myriad, gossamer, thus, pensive* and *whene'er I think of thee.*

Whether it rhymes or not, it seems to me your poetry – if it is to be authentic – has to try and capture something of the spirit of the age; and that means writing in one of the current modes. There are plenty of these. They are not there to choose from, however: in practice I think they choose us.

Shards

If I say we cannot have, for example, 'poetry words' in contemporary poetry, I immediately think of exceptions to the rule. Poetic devices are not just acceptable, they're essential – though they fail if they are obvious. Worn-out technique (such as inversion of word order to eke out a metrical norm or close a rhyme), and, for the same purpose, relying on the short-hand of *oft* and *where'er*: these are sore-thumbs. Likewise, "poetry" expressions – poetry clichés, in fact. Writers use them to try and lift flagging poems – hoping they will inject for instance emotional resonance. They do the reverse. I mentioned *myriad* and *gossamer*. From countless others we might add the ever-popular *shard*. This appeared as long ago as Goldsmith (1730-74) and is still going strong. What is annoying about a shard is that you can go months and not see one anywhere – until you pick up a poetry magazine and suddenly the place is littered with them. One of the ways of positively identifying a poet, in fact, is if s/he's heard of shards. But only if s/he knows what a shard *actually is* is s/he likely to be a good poet.

Language is a living thing. Words' meanings aren't fixed. 'A word exists when two or more people agree to mean the same thing by it,' as Pound says. Pound also said, however, that one of poetry's functions is to 'keep the tools clean', or as Keats has it, 'English must be kept up'. Using poetry clichés ultimately blunts the tools. 'Shard' has lost its original meaning, which was 'a broken piece of earthenware'. Now it just means 'piece' ('shards of glass', etc). So if we really want to say 'shard' now we have to say a 'shard of earthenware'. Interesting to reflect that like gossamer – which was so poetic a word it became a prophylactic – shard is losing its other primary meanings of (i) a beetle's case, and (ii) beetle-dung.

The point I am labouring is that poetry has to be precise. With poetry clichés, it's not just that we're *not* precise but that *we create imprecision.*

Above all and finally on this: to use old-hat devices and "poetry words" is to grasp for an easy effect. At its worst it is like painting by numbers.

Seagulls and teapots: the contemporary idiom

If I am hard on 'shard' I might equally have had a go at the dozens of more sophisticated and up-to-date poetry clichés such as *stippled, lozenge, light* (often a lozenge of – or stippled with – light), *lambent, patina*, and for some reason *seagull*. Why we have so many gulls in poetry these days is a matter for reflection. When you come across a seagull in someone's poem, try substituting the word *teapot*. It is an instructive exercise. And one that brings us back to the spirit of the age.

To be sure, poetry words get into circulation through poetry books. The flamingo principle I alluded to earlier, of writers picking up only surface effects from other poems. But why these particular effects? Why are some words more attractive to us today than others? It is clear I think why we don't find (which Ian McMillan is rooting for) more vests and settees in contemporary poetry. (Poetry is not a classless society, either.) But who can tell why it is that several poets, completely unaware of each other, write simultaneously on the same subject?

A few years ago, foxes were the thing. Ted Hughes and Ted Walker wrote the two most celebrated examples (though there were doubtless many other Teds on with their own). My theory is that, somewhere in the collective unconscious, the fox – drawn as he was in search of food further into towns and cities – became a metaphor for the way people were being drawn from rural to urban life in search of work (as in Ken Smith's long poem *Fox Running*). Well, it's only a theory.

Whatever it was, you should understand that 'the spirit of the age' tends not to deal directly with an issue. The issue as it were deals with the poet. There are people consciously writing for instance about whales and pollution: these are undoubtedly key issues for our time, but do not necessarily represent even a part of the spirit of our age. I wonder if we *can* know what the spirit of the age is until after it has ceased to be.

It need not worry us. Should not worry us. Our job is simply to write the poems. It is for the future to know from our poems – more even than from our novels and documentaries – what it was like to be alive at the close of the twentieth century. If we are not as *pensive* as poets were a hundred years ago, we certainly have more shards. Perhaps they will be the shards of vests beside the stippled patina of so many lambent settees.

FOUR

ALMOST A REMEMBRANCE

Almost a remembrance

When we write vividly and accurately, we create another world for ourselves and our readers. It is a world that comes from within us and is ordered, re-created from things that we already know about the world. It is in this way, I think, that 'memory is mother of the muse'. Yet even in poems taken from life, what we write is not the past but the past re-presented in words. What's more it seems to me something similar is true of the way we re-create the world when we *read* poems. For instance this by William Carlos Williams:

so much depends
upon

a red wheel
barrow

glazed with rain
water

beside the white
chickens.

When I read this poem the detail in it accrues other detail: I see the whitewashed gable-end of a farmhouse, and there – with those chickens pecking round her feet – is a woman bringing washing in off a line. 'No ideas but in things' Williams said. Show us enough and we will fill in the rest: don't philosophise about it, just give us the vivid detail; enough for our imaginations to work with. If his 'wheelbarrow' works for you, it won't be the same as mine, and you won't fill in the same details, but it will carry a similar imaginative charge.

When I first saw that wheelbarrow it seemed to me in Keats's phrase, 'almost a remembrance'. Keats thought good poems did strike us this way. The idea is distinct from Pope's 'What oft was thought but ne'er so well expressed'. We are heirs more to the Romantic than the Classical tradition. The Classicism v. Romanticism ding-dong has been going on, apparently, at least since Aristotle, though Classicism last held sway in Britain in the 18th century, the time of Pope and Co, which is sometimes called the Augustan age (recalling an emperor who died in A.D. 14).

The Augustans valued intellect over emotion, reason over imagination; they wanted elegance with common sense. Which is why many of our sayings derive from the 18th century. For example if Pope could see me rehashing literary history like this he'd point out that a little learning is a dangerous thing and that fools rush in where angels fear to tread.

Another boon for the compiler of books of quotations is Pope's contemporary Dr Johnson. He too was keen on generalisations, saw little value in the particular, local detail, and disliked poets who 'paint each streak on the tulip'. Among Johnson's remarks on writing are: 'No man but a blockhead ever wrote, except for money' and 'the greater part of a writer's time is spent in reading; a man will turn over half a library to write one book'.

Johnson's best-known poem, 'The Vanity of Human Wishes' opens:

Let *Observation* with extensive *View*
Survey Mankind from China to Peru;
Remark each anxious Toil, each eager Strife,
And *watch* the busy Scenes of crouded Life'...

My italics point the redundancies which Wordsworth noted in the Preface to *Lyrical Ballads*. More of a problem I think to us now is that it is impossible to picture Johnson's toil and strife or busy scenes – since they are abstractions. Not a single wheelbarrow in sight. Dr Johnson had other priorities. If we find his poem difficult to appreciate, it is partly that we do not know his classical models, partly that we tend to want poems more to explore than confirm ideas.

In the same Preface, Wordsworth also has it in for Thomas Gray. Gray was chief of the late Augustans, that transitional period against which the Romantics were most strongly to rebel. Here poetry was at its most stylised and furthest from common speech. At its worst, it tended to call a spade an implement for digging ('fish' for instance were 'the finny tribe'). Wordsworth and Coleridge preferred the language of men speaking to men, a tenet which survived modernism and culminated in (as one critic put it) Larkin's 'chaps chatting to chaps'.

The Modernists, working at the beginning of this century, took Wordsworth further, wanting poetry to have the virtues of prose and to assimilate in its imagery and subject matter as much of modern life as it could – 'words that had not been used in poetry before'.

Ezra Pound in 1910 put paid to Dr Johnson's generalisations with one of his own: 'The artist selects and presents the luminous detail. He does not comment.'

In part this exploits the fact that language is not transparent – that the words we use have connotations other than the 'message' they carry. Or which means much the same, but in different words (and so carrying other connotations) this, by John Ash: 'Did you think you could just pick up language and use it, like a spade, the one you call *a spade*.' The artist's comment is in the selection and presentation of the detail.

Practicalities: Show not tell. Speak not recite

The legacies of Romanticism and Modernism are many and not easily put aside. 'Tradition may not be a continuum, and yet it embodies a kind of progression. It is possible to allude to things in it, to take things from it, but to go back is not allowed,' says Michael Schmidt. Which seems a pity, though it absolves us from worrying about 'tradition': it is out of our hands. We cannot go back to Dr Johnson's 'generalities'; or at least not as he recommended. Any neo-Augustanism will have to take account of the 'progression' evinced by the Romantics and Modernists. 'Progression' is imprecise. Poetry is not science and no one has progressed as far as Shakespeare. Nevertheless, poetry has in one sense moved on over the centuries, and we cannot write as if Pound and Eliot never existed. Not, that is, if we are to write authentically, and honour our commitment to the spirit of the age.

The first consequence to draw from all this is that if we are not generalising, then we must 'present the luminous detail': in this way implying what we might otherwise come out and say. We *show* not *tell* (Henry James's dictum). We persuade not insist. Instead of stipulating 'anxious toil' and 'eager strife' we would be more particular: 'disabled by a bulging briefcase / and with his glasses fogged...' Well, my effort is certainly not Dr Johnson, but you get the idea. Above all, this approach allows readers to make up their own minds. They don't have to take our word for it because they are involved in the process.

Why say it again?

One of the most common failings in today's poetry is – as I'm doing here – hammering the point home. The bad poet can't leave it alone, can't respect the reader's intelligence. Worse, he limits his poem by commenting on it. At the end of a poem called 'The Vase' for instance, we might get: 'It slipped from my hands'. An indifferent poet would add, 'and smashed to pieces', and a bad one would add to that, 'It could never be mended'. But it would take a terrible poet to go on with: 'That vase was my life [/our relationship/a symbol of the delicate ecological balance] and now it is shards.'

The 'progression' in our tradition has led to us writing more like speech than 'poetry'. No one would talk about a 'member of the finny tribe'. It's a halibut. And a halibut has the added virtue of being a *specific* member of its tribe.

W.H. Auden apparently defined poetry as 'memorable speech'. Still, poetry is not any old conversation. It is not ordinary but heightened language. We cannot write nowadays what we wouldn't actually say.

But it's worth remembering that we say, in certain circumstances, some pretty remarkable things and in remarkable ways.

What's more, as Schmidt would remind us, though 'poetry can have much to do with speech…even at its most idiomatic it is different in construction both in its rhythmic patterning (however naturally that patterning grows out of speech cadences) and in its semantic intention' [from *Reading Modern Poetry*].

Poet-Speak

Poetry *is* different from speech. But it isn't made different simply by being translated into poet-speak. Again and again writers come up with some rhythmical (or else slap-happy) rehashing of poetical commonplaces, and when anyone asks how they came to write it, they say what the poem might have been: their *talk about* the experience is often much more original, fresh and convincing than the poem itself. Too often the experience, in being turned into a poem, is as it were censored, sanitised.

90% of all poetry is what someone thinks he ought to be writing in the manner he thinks he ought to be writing it.

Craig Raine, formerly poetry editor at Faber and Faber, put it this way: 'Walter Pater and Oscar Wilde both said that all art aspires to the condition of music. They were both wrong. All bad literature aspires to the condition of literature. All good literature aspires to the condition of life. We know that words are only words, but this doesn't mean we shouldn't spend our lives arranging words and choosing words and coining words so that we are deceived by our own illusion of life.'

41

The meaning of life

That heading is from a remark of Blake Morrison's in the *Observer* some years ago. It is also the title of a poem by Ian McMillan, which shows that it's just as easy to call a poem something interesting as it is to call it something dull.

When beginning writers choose the wrong title for a poem, though, it is often because they have approached their subject from the wrong angle. A poem called 'Love' or 'Despair' or even something smaller, like 'Spring', is likely to be much more modest than its title. And it is likely to be very dull indeed. Try and write about The Meaning of Life, as Blake Morrison noted in that article I mentioned, and you will end up staring at a brick wall. Describe a brick wall accurately and you may incidentally say something about the meaning of life.

The McMillan poem, anyway, is subtitled 'A Yorkshire Dialect Rhapsody', and its author is quick to tell northern audiences that it is gibberish, written in response to his being asked, in Surrey, if he ever wrote 'that delightful Yorkshire Dialect poetry'. I used to think that was right, and that it was simply a very funny poem that somehow wasn't like a joke, because it didn't stop being funny. If pressed, I suppose I'd have said it was "really" about how northerners are sometimes portrayed or else perhaps how their language sometimes portrays them. Just now – ten years since I first read it – it struck me that it might be about what its title says it's about.

The Meaning of Life

From under't canal like a watter-filled cellar
coming up like a pitman from a double-un, twice,
I said, 'Hey, you're looking poorly'
He said 'Them nights are drawing in'

Down't stairs like a gob-machine, sucking toffees,
up a ladder like a ferret up a ladder in a fog,
I said 'Hey, you're looking poorly'
He said 'Half-a-dozen eggs'

Over't top in't double-decker groaning like a whippet
like a lamplighter's daughter in a barrel full of milk,
I said 'Hey, you're looking poorly'
He said 'Night's a dozen eggs'

Down't canal like a barrow full of Gillis's parsnips,
coming up like a cage of men in lit-up shiny hats,
I said 'Hey, you're looking poorly'
He said 'Half a dozen nights'

Under't canal on a pushbike glowing like an eggshell
up a ladder wi' a pigeon and a brokken neck,
I said, 'Hey you're looking poorly'
He said 'I feel like half-a-dozen eggs'

Over't night on a shiny bike wi' a lit-up hat,
Perfect for't poorly wi' heads like eggs,
I said 'Hey, you died last week'
He said 'Aye, did you miss me'.

Well, I'm not going to discuss it, that's for sure. Instead I want to
go on to another McMillan poem. This one might have been called
'Mortality' and it is but in a more interesting way:

On the Impossibility of Staying Alive

They have found a new moon;
it stands on my shoulder.
They call it moon because
they lack imagination.
I call it moon because
I lack all conviction.

It has another name
but that name, like God's
is terrible to pronounce.
It is terrible to pronounce
like Czrbrno, a hamlet
in the Balkans. The moon
calls itself moon because
it lacks self-knowledge.

This moon sometimes whispers
and you never heard such rubbish.
I listen because I lack strength,
I smile because I have no muscles
with which to frown. At certain times
of the day, the moon hides.

43

When I am an old man
with flour in my beard, and
packs of incontinence pants
on the sideboard, the moon
will still be new, and will be
perpetually discovered as new
by generations of scientists.
The moon is not a nice man.

Many of McMillan's titles make you want to read the poems: 'Two Miners Pass in Opposite Directions at Daybreak'; 'Simultaneous Evening and Morning'; 'Frosted'; 'From an Evening with The Model of 'The Venus and the Shaving Brushes''' are among my favourites.

Titles can be labels more than a part of the poem. That's OK, but why not then just use the first line as title? Particularly if you run on directly from the title to the *second* line of the poem. For example, *You Brought an Overnight Bag of Everything* continues with the opening line, 'like your bedsocks'.

Some titles use a key word or phrase from the body of the poem, often the clinching last line. Generally it's better to avoid this: a good last line is often pre-empted, like the punchline of a joke; and a key word – containing the theme of the poem for instance – can look striven-for if set at the head of the poem. A way round it is to be a little more oblique. Simon Armitage's title, 'November', gives the poem a context, first of all, but also keys us into its theme.

We walk to the ward from the badly parked car
with your grandma taking four short steps to our two.
We have brought her here to die and we know it.

You check her towel, soap and family trinkets,
pare her nails, parcel her in the rough blankets
and she sinks down into her incontinence.

It is time John. In their pasty bloodless smiles,
In their slack breasts, their stunned brains and their baldness,
and in us John: we are almost these monsters.

You're shattered. You give me the keys and I drive
through the twilight zone, past the famous station
to your house, to numb ourselves with alcohol.

Inside, we feel the terror of dusk begin.
Outside we watch the evening, failing again,
and we let it happen. We can say nothing.

Sometimes the sun spangles and we feel alive.
One thing we have to get, John, out of this life.

It might have been called 'On the Impossibility of Staying Alive'. Incontinence features in both poems to represent not only the loss of dignity, but also of course the powerlessness in ageing. In Ian McMillan's poem it is something unspeakable – or at least not spoken: 'terrible to pronounce'. And in our secular world it is not the name of God but a language joke which sustains us, 'terrible to pronounce like Czrbrno'.

The moon is not a romantic image, but something indifferent and terrible which endures beyond us, renewing itself. Some people – 'They' – call it moon because they lack imagination: they cannot or dare not imagine what 'the impossibility of staying alive' means. Byron said, 'And if I laugh at any mortal thing / 'Tis that I may not weep.' So it is with Ian McMillan, who has 'no muscles / with which to frown'. Something of that 'moon' – what it represents – also appears in the Armitage poem, but there it is in the word-play of 'It is time'. Time to leave the hospital, time to leave grandma to it, but also of course time which is 'in us' too: which is making us 'almost these monsters'. The 'I' of the poem and his friend John – all of us – are subject to the dusk beginning.

There is plenty more to be said about the poems, but I want to draw your attention to their endings. It is tempting to finish a poem with a flourish, but the bigger the ending the more it has to have been *earned* by what precedes it.

On the other hand, throwaway last lines can be wearing, making the poem like a shaggy-dog story. The endings in these two both make statements, are summings-up. Neither are grandiloquent, though the Armitage sounds it, lacking McMillan's humour. As it happens, Armitage has said that he lifted the last line of 'November' (which he found 'highly philosophical for Hollywood and worth having') from a 70s cowboy series, *Alias Smith and Jones*, spoken by the lead characters as they ride through the opening credits. That information surely changes the way we read that last line. For one thing, it adds another touch of detail.

Why the last lines of these two poems work, for me, is that like their titles they are oblique without being vague, suggestive without being narrow. It's not that you can't define what they mean – and quite precisely – but that they will always mean more than your definition.

Meaning?

I suppose I have discussed these poems to show how writers can deal with a "big subject" without tackling it head on. Their different titles for identical themes are pointers to their very different treatments. It is easy in our writing – and our reading – to want a poem's meaning to be up-front, obvious, dealt with in a clear-cut way. This invariably limits the poem (though poems needn't be puzzles). Poems aren't 'about' something per se. They aren't philosophy or they'd have been written in discursive prose. As Shelley has it 'nothing can equally be expressed in prose that is not tedious and superogatory in verse'. And usually poems are of course – like the two I've just scratched the surface of – "about" several things at the same time. In her book *Mystery and Manners*, Flannery O'Connor makes a point about short stories which is true of poems too, that they are not 'abstract meaning but experienced meaning'.

The meaning of a story has to be embodied in it, has to be made concrete in it. A story is a way to say something that can't be said any other way, and it takes every word in the story to say what the meaning is. You tell a story because a statement would be inadequate. When anyone asks what a story is about the only proper thing is to tell him to read the story. The meaning of the fiction is not abstract meaning but experienced meaning, and the purpose of making statements about the meaning of a story is only to help you experience that meaning more fully.

Titles needn't be just a picture hook to hang the poem on. They can welcome us into a poem. And they can contain information we need to understand it. Call a monologue 'Despair' and we start very little wiser, but 'Margaret Thatcher on the Occasion of Her Fall from Office' clues us up immediately. (You could of course keep 'Despair' and have the other line as epigraph. But the title is an advert for the poem.)

The scenic route

Some titles come first and suggest the poem. This is surely true for instance of the John Ashbery piece entitled 'Untilted'. But I'd say that the 'message' ought not to come before the poem. If we are determined to say something and sit down to write it, we will not enter into a contract with language but simply bully it to our ends. And then, for its part, language will tend to subvert our attempt by letting us deal only in stock phrases and stock routines to prompt stock responses. Clearly, some writers do set out to get a message across, but if they are successful they work with the medium, allow themselves to be surprised by the way patterns of imagery, assonance and alliteration, for example, generate unexpected directions. They start out for Brighton and certainly they get there, but they go via Oslo. Ian McMillan's habitually "difficult" procedures had to be laid aside while writing about the Miners' Strike in his *Tall in the Saddle* poems; but the plainer style is still recognisably his.

The next poem I want to look at is by Carol Ann Duffy. She has been praised by Peter Porter as 'a crusading sensibility refusing to surrender any touch of art to the urgency of its cause'. A friend told her how ladies' maids were often obliged to wear their mistresses' pearls during the day's work, since body heat improved the pearls' appearance (in time for the evening ball). The friend expected Duffy to be outraged. In fact she found the image erotic.

Warming Her Pearls

Next to my own skin, her pearls. My mistress
bids me wear them, warm them, until evening
when I'll brush her hair. At six, I place them
round her cool, white throat. All day I think of her,

resting in the Yellow Room, contemplating silk
or taffeta, which gown tonight? She fans herself
whilst I work willingly, my slow heat entering
each pearl. Slack on my neck, her rope.

She's beautiful. I dream about her
in my attic bed; picture her dancing
with tall men, puzzled by my faint, persistent scent
beneath her French perfume, her milky stones.

I dust her shoulders with a rabbit's foot,
watch the soft blush seep through her skin
like an indolent sigh. In her looking-glass
my red lips part as though I want to speak.

Full moon. Her carriage brings her home. I see
her every movement in my head... Undressing,
taking off her jewels, her slim hand reaching
for the case, slipping naked into bed, the way

she always does... And I lie here awake,
knowing the pearls are cooling even now
in the room where my mistress sleeps. All night
I feel their absence and I burn.

'I work willingly,' she says; but in the next line: 'Slack on my neck,
her rope': a string of pearls is called a rope, so the metaphorical
implications – halter, noose – don't get in the way of the poem,
qualified as they are by the fact that the rope is 'slack' and that
her own 'heat enter[s] / each pearl'. Stanza four is clearly erotic
and political; especially in the last line and a half: 'In her looking-
glass / my red lips part as though I want to speak.' Again the poet
manages to get the literal before the figurative: 'looking-glass' is of
course what they'd call a mirror in those days. It shows the maid
as though she wants to speak; but she has no voice: she is only a
maid, after all. Equally – you notice the poet bothers to note '*red*
lips part' – her love is speechless too.

I have known people read this poem with no notion – until it
was pointed out – that 'Warming Her Pearls' is a love poem. As a
matter of fact we have the poet's word for it; though I know that
we can't always trust what the poet says.

Love and fruit

My guess is that all good poems to some extent surprise their authors.
We may write a chaste love poem which includes a mango for
instance and only years later realise what is going on as it were
under the surface, what part of our imaginative experience we are
accessing, how different it would have been had it been a banana.

Christina Rossetti's longish narrative *Goblin Market* seems today
quite explicit in its sexuality, though it was often given to children
to learn by heart as a fairy tale. Lizzie calls to Laura:

48

'Come and kiss me.
Never mind my bruises,
Hug me, kiss me, suck my juices
Squeezed from goblin fruits for you,
Goblin pulp and goblin dew.
Eat me, drink me, love me...'

It is easy to see why *Goblin Market* has been read recently as a proto-feminist text; and few can doubt that Rossetti intended something of the sort, with its ending:

For there is no friend like a sister
In calm or stormy weather;
To cheer one on the tedious way,
To fetch one if one goes astray,
To lift one if one totters down,
To strengthen whilst one stands.

How far she was aware of the entendres in the imagery and so on is debatable. The anthology I quote it from was first published in 1921, by which time the poem was already something of a minor classic. The anthology's back cover has the assurance: 'This collection does not make great demands on the reader by introducing "difficult" poetry that has introspective meaning or obscure language.' Rossetti's poem has had (at least) one life and today has another. The way it was originally understood gave the poem celebrity and prominence – and therefore made it available (unlike its now forgotten contemporaries) to our age's reappraisal. And reading it now, post-Freud, makes it a different poem altogether; though some may feel that there is something more post-Benny Hill in interpreting such lines as 'She dreamed of melons'.

It's worth comparing *Goblin Market* with Coleridge's *Christabel*, incidentally, which deals with a similar theme. One warning though about this area. Updating fairytales has had a vogue lately. Unless you have an unstoppable idea, I'd not bother with doing any myself for a while. Nowadays all too often the prince and princess / live happily ever / after their divorce.

FIVE

WRITING POEMS

Adjectives, adverbs, that sort of thing

We are suspicious of adjectives. Especially two adjectives (or adverbs) where one would do; or where, if you just had the right noun or verb, you wouldn't need any at all. "Describing words" don't only describe but *tell* us what to think. What's more, these "intensifiers" are also *qualifiers* and sometimes the unqualified expression is the more intense one. 'I love you very much indeed' is nice. But 'I love you' comes from the heart.

Strike it out

Dr Johnson said something shrewd when he advised writers to: 'Read over your compositions and where ever you meet a passage which you think is particularly fine, strike it out.' Ezra Pound said something a little similar, though less drastic, to Basil Bunting: that sometimes, although a line is quite brilliant in itself, it does not suit the poem. You can always use it elsewhere, of course.

Equally, there's no room for the dull or inconsequential word/ line/image. If something's not working *for* the poem, it is working *against* it. Can you say the same thing more concisely or/and more interestingly? Does it need saying at all? It's true that a poem has to have light and shade, but on the whole it's best to remember the advice Keats gave to Shelley (though Shelley seems to have disregarded it), that 'you might be more of an artist and load every vein with ore'.

Telling the truth

Write an autobiographical novel and people will suspect you couldn't do a 'real' work of fiction. Pen a love poem, however, and the reader is appalled if it's not true. What does this tell us? Well, you know I think a poem should be true.

Auden in the Foreword to his *Collected Shorter Poems* explained that he had dropped some pieces because they were 'dishonest':

A dishonest poem is one which expresses, no matter how well, feelings or beliefs which its author never felt or entertained. For example, I once expressed a desire for 'New styles of architecture': but I have never liked modern architecture. I prefer *old* styles, and one should be honest even about one's prejudices.

The impulse or emotion behind the poem should be true, even if the facts are made up.

The reverse of which is that if we don't believe you it's no good saying 'but this actually happened'. Poems that are false to an emotion omit detail or, more often, clutter their stanzas with abstract statements that 'tell not show'. Sometimes, too, with detail which is irrelevant or in a different tone to the rest of the poem. This is often either borrowed ('poetry') language, or else detail in its raw state: material which has not been internalised, sifted by the imagination – transmuted into poetry. It lies on the page, inert. Anyone can put down 'what actually happened': you have to do it so that *it happens again* whenever anyone reads your poem. So. It is not about giving the facts. What *are* the *facts* after all? Surely only the facts as you saw them. A poem based on a conversation between two people might work best as a monologue; a poem may conflate three separate Sundays into one; and, if you need a rhyme, an incident in July might better occur in June...Or maybe not.

Lies

'The apple rotted quietly among the leaves.'
'The sweet sugar rotted our love.'
'The sky was black as a rotted plank.'

Things have gone wrong in all three of these statements. In the first, 'quietly' is synaesthesia – expressing one sense in terms of another. But it isn't convincing because in this context it is only intended to soften the verb, and it does rather more than that: the word 'quietly' can't help bringing along the idea of sound, and is in fact louder than having nothing there at all.

The second poet wanted to point the metaphor in 'sugar', so stressed its sweetness. But it is generally best to get the surface meaning right and let the other meanings take care of themselves. Don't come in between your poem and what it is saying: let it speak for itself. It is silly to say sweet sugar – what other sort is there? Though sweet *wine* would be palatable here because you'd be specifying (whatever the underlying metaphor) that it is not *dry*. And sugar rotting love? Rotting your teeth, more likely, at which point your partner might call it a day, gummy. The real problem for me is that the idea is over-direct: it tells us, and it tells us rather obviously.

The third image was probably suggested by context, which I imagine to be a poem about a dilapidated shed. I don't like it because the simile draws attention to itself or rather to the poet: 'aren't I clever for thinking up such an unusual image?' It's great to have surprising images if they're apt and if they're in service of the poem. A plank has texture and smell and even rotted is in fact rarely *black*.

Typographical crimes

Head of my hit-list is a very minor misdemeanour and in some hands no misdemeanour at all: the lowercase 'i'. Some say it is more modest than the usual capitalised 'I'. In practice, it is startling. Offending against the general usage, in effect it shouts 'look at i!' 'i' was popular a few decades ago, though only in poems. Often poems with typographical effects that seem gauche&oldhat if you try and use them now.

the lowercase poem is similarly irritating. starting a sentence with a lowercase looks odd unless you've got a good reason for it. On the 'Should poems begin their lines with an uppercase letter?' question, my position is It's up to you. Whichever seems to fit that particular poem best. Generally, I think free-verse looks odd with capitals heading the lines. Whereas the more traditional forms may gain from it. The only thing to remember is that capitals add a little extra emphasis to the line break.

More serviceable I think   than lowercase throughout   because less stylised   is the poem without punctuation   This often uses extra bar spaces   to denote the pause normally afforded by com-mas   full stops and so on

Which brings me to remark that, if you're getting, say, cluttered up with commas, you can, with profit, drop some of the punctu-ation – the line-endings do the job for you.

Absence of punctuation and tricksy
line and stanza
breaks can be
effective   Lineation
is discussed elsewhere but note
the movements of
emphasis and make sure
any ambiguities are fruit
-ful not wilful just there
for the sake of it.

Boring

More often than you'd think, poets try to justify boring writing by saying 'It's about Sunday afternoon' or 'If you'd *been at* the last home match...' Either you don't write about something that's boring (or dull or clumsy or in some other way bad) or you have to do it supremely well.

I do not mean that poems need be 'entertainments'. I do not mean for a moment that you should write with the intention of entertaining your audience. But there is no virtue in being dull. Good poems, however difficult their form and however unexciting or intractable their material, are always readable. There is something about them that makes us go back and read them. We know that they will the repay effort. Boring poems ask more of the reader than the poem can offer; and generally that is because the writer hasn't done enough work or the right sort of work.

You should not write for your audience. But imagine that 60-line poem about your Grandma was actually by someone else. Try reading it as if you'd never seen it before. Which bits are more complicated than they need to be? Which bits are 'all right but so what'?

If you were in the slightest bit bored when *writing* that poem, then the poem will almost certainly be boring. However, if you were so excited that you couldn't be bothered to watch what you were doing, then you have also almost certainly written a boring poem.

We get lazy. We get an idea and then expect to find it written up for us in our notebooks; or else, half-way through, our concentration wanders, and we let it go slack. Effort on our part isn't the same as being boring. Being lazy usually is.

'Writing poetry is more than anything else an attitude of mind' Stanley Cook once said. A person's attitude usually says more about how good a poet they are (or will be) than what they have actually written. Most poets are bad poets because they are not interested in poetry, only in their own writing, and not really in that. I know too many beginning writers who get stuck because of their attitude. It is terrible to see. They tend to write the kind of poetry that makes you want to hit them.

The Disaster Poem

Whenever something terrible happens which occasions national grief or outrage, thousands of people write bad poems about it. Some of these writers even upbraid others for not writing bad poems about it themselves. Which is, I think, to misunderstand the function of poetry, and confuses civic and political responsibilities with artistic ones.

I was faced in Doncaster once with a poem entitled 'Aberfan', around the 25th anniversary of that tragedy. My heart sank. But in fact it was a fine poem and genuinely moving. And the reason was this, that it was based on personal experience. It wasn't the reaction of someone watching TV or listening to the radio, and it didn't arrogate to itself the role of 'speaking for the people'. I've not been able to find the poem again, so I can't quote it, but the feeling behind the poem has stayed with me. Twenty-five years before, the poet was a young mother, living in the next valley to Aberfan; the poem tells how she had sent her children off to school through yet another morning of torrential rain. Later she hears the news bulletin. At first she believes her children are in danger, possibly killed. Then comes the relief, almost joy. And then the guilt: which is, finally, what the poem is about; not, in any direct sense, 'Aberfan' at all.

Mouths

Cousin to the Disaster is the Issue Poem. In this too it is easy to use the material to disguise or shore up indifferent writing. I once had to review an anthology of CND verse. In politics I tend just to the left of 'Put me down as not bothered' but these poems brought out the militant in me. Sloppy, clumsy, cliché-ridden, and original only in their spelling and every now and then a stunning mixed metaphor. What the poems showed me was that the issues they raised mattered to me and that these writers were trivialising and travestying their cause. Writing about an issue underlines the saying that we all have a responsibility to our poems.

Ciaran Carson has a sequence of poems which includes:

The Mouth

There was this head had this mouth he kept shooting off.
  Unfortunately.
It could have been worse for us than it was for him.
  Provisionally.
But since nothing in this world is certain and you don't know
  who hears what
We thought it was time he bit off more than he could chew.
  Literally.
By the time he is found there'll be nothing much left to tell
  who he was.

But of course some clever dick from the 'Forensic Lab'
    reconstructs
Him, what he used to be – not from his actual teeth, not his
    fingerprints,
But from the core – the toothmarks of the first and last bite
    he'd taken of
This sour apple. But then we would have told them anyway.
    Publicity.

This seems to me savagely controlled. It does not present 'the issue' but an experience from it. The voice Carson borrows here is calm, amused, determined, awful. The poem contrasts demotic speech and the balancing short lines. The rhyme scheme in the first stanza is broken round 'Literally' and 'who hears what' and 'who he was', suggesting how important those ideas are to each other. The last word closes the poem completely, while leaving us to consider 'the issues' for ourselves.

Now here is a poem by John Ash. It is no less urgent in dealing with its "issues", lyrical, inventive, beautiful though it is. What do you think killed the neighbour? Who is being addressed at the end of the poem? It may help to know that the poem was written only a few years ago in New York.

Smoke

It was late in the year
and forests were burning a long way off,
the day the smoke arrived, almost unperceived.
It came as a ghost, as many ghosts,
visible in the mouths of tunnels.

Now that your neighbour is dead,
you recall casual greetings on the stairs,
snatches of show tunes in the corridors,
and you look down into that well –

that well of uncertain light and air – and see an absence
which neither snow nor corrosive rain efface,
and the absence returns your glance, it follows like a cur
extending its tongue of smoke toward your hand.

The smoke enters the lamplight and the bed.
The eyes are clouded, the eyes are abolished,
and the ears that drank in the old arias of desire.
Venice is diminished, and Rome,

their bells dulled, their restaurants emptied;
in Manhattan the towers shrink from the sky;
all places and all scenes become the less observed,
the less heard, the less loved.

In a city of burnt throats there can never be
enough sweet water to start the songs
and if you would dance, you must dance to the memory
of that lighted window the dusk carried off,

those hands preparing the evening meal,
skeletal hands fumbling among
the bottles of useless prophylactics,
those limbs and mouths, smoke we daily breathe.

But don't vanish, don't take the path to the river.
It is cold there and lonely,
and the sky is a burnt page. Stay –

you and you others. If we are not to become
a dispersed people of smoke,
the monument that is us must be built soon.

And as a contrast to that, I want to quote a poem by Geoff Hattersley. I think it is about "protest" in its way, and about writing poems.

Christmas Shopping, Sheffield

You were writing dud cheques
like no one's business,
I was splashing
the forged tenners around.

In the Hole in the Road
someone sang
'Take Me To Tulsa',
snow settling on his sombrero.

56

I tossed him a tenner
screwed into a ball.

A woman approached,
armed with documents
and truth;
she was selling badges,
a definite bargain
at a tenner apiece.

I signed the petition
to end Apartheid,
I do a lot
of possibly useless writing.

The final poem in this section, by Tom Leonard, makes its point literally in the way it is written. The speech here is Glaswegian: try reading it aloud exactly as it is spelt.

Unrelated Incidents (3)

this is thi
six a clock
news thi
man said n
thi reason
a talk wia
BBC accent
iz coz yi
widny wahnt
mi ti talk
aboot thi
trooth wia
voice lik
wanna yoo
scruff. if
a toktaboot
thi trooth
lik wanna yoo
scruff yi
widny think
it wuz troo.

jist wanna yoo
scruff tokn.
thirza right
way ti spell
ana right way
ti tok it. this
is me tokn yir
right way a
spellin. this
is ma trooth.
yooz doant no
thi trooth
yirsellz cawz
yi canny talk
right. this is
the six a clock
nyooz. belt up.

Leonard is a fine reader of his work, and his dialect poems are tremendous in performance. For me, though, they are even more effective on the page, because they force the reader to take on the narrator's voice, to speak the poems in that voice. There's a sudden moment of understanding, when a phrase gives up its meaning; that moment of "translation" seems to me to exemplify what happens in a great deal of poetry – though it is not always so literally a translation. We suddenly "get it", whether that is an isolated connection like the punchline of a joke or something more diffuse in a poem overall. I would guess that all good poems leave space in one form or another for a reader to make a leap of understanding.

Conscious and unconscious

Who knows how that leap of understanding occurs? Who knows, for that matter, what similar processes are at work when we're writing a poem? We can't know while we're doing it, otherwise we wouldn't be doing it – because so much to do with writing occurs in the unconscious, as it were despite ourselves. Working consciously on a poem can be like when a name is on the tip of your tongue; the more you search, the further you push it down your throat. There is a point to working consciously on a poem, though; for one thing, you don't know when you may rekindle the original inspiration and begin writing well again. But also, even if you don't improve the poem you're working on, what you learn from that process may well inform the next poem you write.

The best poems can come easily and pretty much of-a-piece. When you're writing well, it's as though someone else is doing it for you, someone who has found what you need to say and how to say it. You trust the process. You trust everything that you've learned so far, every relevant thing you've done, thought, read, experienced. That's all it takes: trust. A painter who knows she needs some red in the bottom left hand corner puts a pillar-box in there. It might have been a fire-engine or a sports car but the subject somehow dictated against them. She doesn't quite know why the pillar-box is there, it just feels right. It is for the art-critic to point out that first of all the red balances a red elsewhere in the painting; and then to say that the pillar-box represents "communication".

Think about *Hamlet*. Did Shakespeare really mean all that? In one sense he can't have. If he'd worked out all the layers and connections, he'd still be scratching his head over the 'To be or not to be' bit. Even much of the overall structuring will have been done, I think, unconsciously. When you are writing well, you are working too fast to "think". You make decisions, of course, conscious decisions on phrasing and so on – it is not just taking dictation (though very occasionally it seems like it). So, though it is never entirely a passive process – poets are "makers" after all – you make the *right* decisions and you do so without much, if any, deliberation. I want to stress this. Many potentially good poems fail because their author just didn't do enough with them, so that they stay directionless, or heading the wrong way, or cluttered up, or burdened down, or are simply trying to cover too much territory. Randall Jarrell despaired over writers who had hundreds of poems but who 'had never *made* a poem'.

Still, this is not the same as working consciously on a poem or to a formula. Any fairly intelligent person can put together a poem that has all the requisite parts and does not live. Which brings me to talk about

Drafting

A poem can take several radically different drafts to arrive at a finished version. A poem can inch forward, draft after draft to show you what you are trying to say. And every poem, with whatever certainty it arrives, will need some adjustment. A word too many here, a phrase out of tone there, a stanza that would be better higher

59

up the poem or dropped altogether. This sort of editing can be done cold. For more extensive drafting, it seems to me you need to be in as heightened a creative state as when you wrote the poem originally. If you do this surgery with your conscious mind, or in the wrong creative mood, there is a danger of killing the patient. Drafting can be in effect quarrying an old poem to make a new one.

Each of us finds our own way in this. Sharing the poem can help. A friend or workshop's feedback can identify symptoms if not offer a true diagnosis. Beware of sharing it too soon, however. Sometimes that can cripple a poem, just as "talking out" a poem frequently stops it getting written.

Workshops are pretty much the most useful place in the world for a poet. But they can encourage polishing – 'take these words out and you're fine' – rather than redrafting. As Ian McMillan puts it, 'The poem's tie gets straightened when it needs a whole new wardrobe.'

The creative process

In 1926, working from the observations of several creative thinkers, Graham Wallace came up with a theory which has been generally accepted as plausible. He sees the creative process as taking four stages: Preparation; Incubation; Illumination; Verification.

Preparation is when you find and then consider the problem from all angles. For the poet it is when you get an idea or a line or an image or just the feeling that you need to write about something. You may brainstorm and you may do research and you may work consciously, pushing words around. You may do no writing at all. It's also the stage, and this is important, when you have to decide if the idea for the poem is really workable. Sometimes you decide the idea really isn't up to much after all, or else maybe that *you* aren't up to *it*. Making that decision now can save you a lot of time. As long as you are aware that some poems will disregard your decision and make sure you write them anyway.

Incubation. This stage reminds me of the Roger McGough poem that begins, 'It's like bashing your head against a brick wall, / sighed the Bishop, / bashing my head against a brick wall.' You've reached a point where the poem just doesn't seem to be coming together, so you give up and do something else. The theory goes that the unconscious now takes over.

Illumination. This is when the poem is ready to be written. Something has happened to sort the ideas out for you, to give you the central image you need, to suggest the form, whatever. You write the poem or, as I say, sometimes the poem writes itself.

Verification is looking at the poem with an editor's eye, revising as necessary, deciding if what was genius late Thursday night is yet another poem about Autumn on Friday morning and badly written to boot. You may have to start all over again.

These stages are an abstraction. We don't know how the creative process works. Sometimes it seems all the stages happen pretty much at once; sometimes it may be that we don't realise we've already done the 'preparation'. Sometimes the 'incubation' stage happens in bits and pieces. Often all four stages happen in miniature and as it were on fast-forward. If you're the sort of writer who breaks off continually to make coffee and later to go to the loo, these two procedures probably have more to do with each other than the obvious: you are giving your unconscious mind time to deal with the conscious creative problem. Likewise when, sitting down to work, you get up again to tidy round and do the washing up you've left for days. It's not prevaricating, it's being an artist. However, a number of people have noticed that the "given" poem – the *donné* – happens more often when you're working hard on something else – prose for instance – and rarely when you're just sitting with your feet up waiting for inspiration.

Sitting with your feet up (or in Keats's phrase, 'diligent indolence') is certainly essential. But don't overdo it. Even though we are now going on to:

Dreaming

'Poems are like dreams, in them you put what you don't know you know' – Adrienne Rich.

I don't want to be too high-flown about this, but let's not forget that poems are special things. All we have do is write, it's true. But still, there are times when we write better than we can, better in a sense than we are. 'One needs to allow poems to speak for their moment,' Adrienne Rich says. Interestingly, she goes on to say that 'the meaning of a poem becomes clear to me only as I see what happens in my life; poems are more like premonitions than conclusions.'

Not all poems are journeys of discovery (and some that are take us places only a dimbo would want to visit); but writing does tend to surprise us in smaller or larger ways – be that with an insight or a piece of information or simply just a word 'we didn't know we knew'.

Poems are not dreams, though they can be written with the sureness of purpose of a somnambulist, and occasionally written as if they were, like dreams, 'strange pictures/and signs scribbling themselves':

Nocturne

I drive through a village at night, the houses rise up
in the glare of my headlights – they're awake, want to drink.
Houses, barns, signs, ownerless dogs – it's now
they clothe themselves in Life. – The people are sleeping:

some can sleep peacefully, others have drawn features
as if training hard for eternity.
They don't dare let go though their sleep is heavy.
They rest like lowered crossing-barriers when the mystery draws
        past.

Outside the village the road goes far among the forest trees.
And the trees the trees keeping silence in concord with each
        other.
They have a theatrical colour, like firelight.
How distinct each leaf! They follow me right home.

I lie down to sleep, I see strange pictures
and signs scribbling themselves behind my eyelids
on the wall of the dark. Into the slit between wakefulness and
        dream
a large letter tries to push itself in vain.

TOMAS TRANSTRÖMER, *translated from the Swedish by Robin Fulton*

Other poems are less like somnambulism as that awake and alert concentration of driving at night. You get to the end of the poem only dimly aware of the landscape you've travelled through, the route you've expertly navigated. I know that sometimes, and more often perhaps, writing a poem is more like driving in thick fog! And I see my metaphors are getting me on thin ice. But where I'm heading with them is that we learn to trust that night road, we learn to trust our driving, simply by practice. By what Flannery O'Connor calls 'the habit of art'. That is, reading, writing, and Keats's 'watchfulness in itself'. O'Connor puts it this way:

Art is the habit of the artist; and habits have to be rooted deep in the whole personality. They have to be cultivated like any other habit, over a long period of time, by experience; and teaching any kind of writing is largely a matter of helping the student develop the habit of art. I think this is more than just a discipline, although it is that; I think it is a way of looking at the created world and of using the senses so as to make them find as much meaning as possible in things.

*

I want to circle round to dreams again, and to what Les Murray has to say about them. In an essay, 'Poems and Poesies', he talks about 'the aesthetic experience', which, in its verbal form, 'is what people mean when they ask how much poetry a text has got in it...

It is that in a book or a piece of verse that can't be summarised or put into other words; we feel a constraint about doing so, a feeling that we would violate something. Where the experience is intense, we find it extremely attractive, fascinating, and yet quickly exhausting; we want it, and more of it, but we have to take frequent rests from it: if we stay focussed on it...it will itself seem to come and go. It is an experience we can have repeatedly, but find it hard to take in steadily, to sustain. The realms of gold, it would seem, oscillate – or our mind does, when we behold them.
   In another way, though, and this is perhaps even more striking in cases where the intensity is not so high, poetry has an odd quality of inexhaustibility. We can experience it, go away from it, analyse it, try to order it tidily among the other phenomena of our life – but as soon as we come back to it and quiet down in its presence, as even a low-intensity piece of real poetry will make us do, we find it to be as mysterious and pregnant with elusive significance as ever...We don't exhaust the aesthetic experience; it exhausts us, or at least our manoeuvres and calculations.

He goes on to make a connection between the 'oscillations' of the aesthetic experience, and 'the two modes of consciousness, one for waking life and one for dreaming'. The one is said by psychologists to relate to the recently evolved forebrain, the other to the older so-called limbic levels of the brain, sometimes called the reptilian brain:

As people knew in ancient times, and as we have known since Freud...neither of our two lives is wholly subordinate to the other – or if it is, we're likely to be in trouble. For ordinary mental health, let alone any sort of fullness of life, we need a measure of harmony between them. The aesthetic experience, I suggest, presents us with this harmony in a heightened, sometimes supremely heightened way. It is a fusion of the two, and delivers us into wholeness of thinking and of life. Or at least it models that wholeness vividly for us.

Just as Coleridge warns about misusing the potency of metre, Murray notes that though we must have something of this 'dream', or else writing may seem dead, lifeless or prosey: 'On the other hand, too much of this dream atmosphere without corresponding rational strengths is apt to strike us as suspect, and explains the resistance of a great many people to all but very good examples of surrealism...' [from *The Paperbark Tree*].

*

The curious smoke

To pause now on a less charged note, here is a witty, nicely-edged poem where Evangeline Paterson makes use of the idea of 'singing what we see':

Literary Portrait

He can make fire
with his finger-ends

and into it go
letters he is sent
gifts he is given
people trees buildings

and in the curious
drifting smoke
he sings what he sees.

There is no one who sings
like him. Listen

but keep your distance.
He needs
a great deal of fuel.

We see/what we write/what we see through that 'curious drifting smoke' of our experience. Looking more often, you learn to see more clearly. Reading more, you read more fully. Writing a word prompts other words, sentences breed sentences.

Inspiration often comes in cycles, and generally accompanies or follows periods when you are reading well (reading in such a way that the poem becomes three-dimensional). Everyone has dry or fallow periods, but it's good practice, I think, to write as regularly as you can, even if that means having to tip the dustbin men a bit more at Christmas.

Joining a group can give you the framework – the routine and the discipline – as well as the stimulus to keep reading and writing. And so, on to the next section.

WORKSHOP TECHNIQUES
AND WRITING GAMES

Workshops

I said earlier that everyone should try a workshop once: I meant one that suited you, tried over a period of time. Ask at your library or ring your Regional Arts Board for your nearest group.

There are several kinds. The most common is where writers read out their work and discuss it together. Another is where people actually write in the session. A third – rarer – is a *class* where principles of writing are expounded by a teacher, examples brought in, and exercises are set. Ideally I think you want something of all three.

Another distinction is how far the group is democratic. Is there a leader? If so is s/he a teacher or a facilitator?

Even a bad workshop can be a lifeline when you're starting. The important thing is that you enjoy going to the group and feel you're getting somewhere. A general writing workshop can be interesting, though there is rarely much crossover between the genres: often even accomplished fiction writers know very little about poetry. And that may include the workshop leader.

Don't judge the group too soon: the learning process is circuitous and it's easy to underestimate people. However, I follow Jocky Wilson (talking about darts) that if your team doesn't move up each season, and you don't feel you're improving, then you have to join another. (Not necessarily *instead* of the one you're with, of course, especially if it adjourns to the pub.) Workshops are not infrequently wonderful places. But in many of them writers go years learning nothing or worse.

You need a group who can see what you're trying to do, and what is genuine in your work, and who will judge it in those terms. And of course who will encourage you to better things. The waving of an editorial scalpel is not always more use than blanket praise; neither is as necessary as learning discrimination and sorting out what makes poems work.

To this end I'd personally like to see more groups discussing published poets. I don't mean as students to pass exams, and still less in the spirit of those old "poetry appreciation" classes. I want them to look at these poets as fellow practitioners, going to poems to further their own writing through developing new enthusiasms and exploring new procedures and perspectives. The best way I've found is to begin each workshop session with 'this week's poet': two or three poems in photocopy handed round, read out a couple of times and then discussed in some detail. Of course this may involve the tutor doing a certain amount of homework! Group members – not just the tutor – should be encouraged to choose these featured poets too (and to lead the discussion).

All writers I believe can be guided towards more authentic writing, though each of us develops in our own way and at our own pace.

It may be you have to travel some distance to find the workshop that suits you. It may be that you have to start your own.

Workshop techniques and writing games

Most of the exercises detailed below may be used as starting points for solo writing, though they are set out for use in a group. If you've joined a workshop that doesn't write in the session, you might ask the tutor and other members whether they'd like to give it a go. In which case you must get the tutor to buy a copy of this book, since you won't want to part with yours.

Before we go any further though, I want to say a few things about writing games. The first is simply this, that in my experience writers almost always improve as a result of using them. It is easy to dismiss them as artificial, and I would admit that the process is often more important than the product. Even so, many fine poems have been begun – some actually completed – as exercises. It does not matter what has prompted the poem if the writing is genuine: there are times, whatever the workshop task, when you are ready to write well. It is then that – even if you are writing in the voice of a kangaroo – your imagination becomes genuinely engaged and you start to process material which really matters to you.

What's more, there is a certain energy generated when writing as part of a group, which often forces a poem into being – one that would not have got written at home. It is a fortunate paradox that no one expects you to write well under direction, and so it is often actually easier to access the areas of your imagination that help you to say what needs to be said. You are more able to trust the process and discover what Eliot calls the 'passive attendence upon events' necessary to all good writing. Put another way, you don't have time to worry about the blank page: the exercise provides you with a structure and a purpose.

Eliot believed that the chief use of 'meaning' in some poems is 'to satisfy one habit of the reader, to keep his mind diverted and quiet, while the poem does its work upon him.' I think something similar is true for the writer using a workshop game. Eliot again: 'The bad poet is usually unconscious where he ought to be conscious, and conscious where he ought to be unconscious.' There is nothing like a writing game for rendering you unconscious. The most important thing, using these games, is not to become *self-conscious*.

Adapt the examples below to suit you. Invent your own.

FREE WRITING (also called hot-penning). The mainstay of any writing session. Use as a warm-up and as an exercise in itself. You give the group a line, which they write down and continue writing from. There are three rules:

1) Once you've started you must not stop writing.
2) You must not think. Let the writing go its own way – as far from the starting point as you like. This is not a "considered" piece.
3) You must not rhyme. (Rhyme is a constraint.)

Stress that they cannot get this wrong – unless they chew their pens. They *must* write, however inconsequential, daft or odd it is. If they get stuck they can write 'I'm stuck, I'm stuck' over and over, or note down things they see in the room, until the writing comes free again.

No one should be obliged to read back. People will be less inhibited this way; and it is quite common to uncover very personal and vulnerable material. On the other hand, this writing works so well partly from the pressure of knowing most *will* read back.

Your starting line should be open. Something short will do: 'When he came in'; 'It started to rain'; 'I knew it would go wrong'; 'The house was empty'; 'In the distance'. Sometimes it is worth giving a context, 'a holiday' for example, or an additional task which may suggest context – having them include given words, like 'library' or 'milkshake'. First lines from existing poems are useful – and afterwards you may wish to read the original. Naturally, a line with a strong metre may prompt writing that is in that metre.

It's often worth asking your writers to close their eyes and clear their minds before you start. Tell them how long they've got: anything from two to ten minutes; but make sure everyone keeps writing, even if they think they've 'finished'. Give warning when you're about to stop them: 'One minute'. Let individuals continue writing if they like while the rest read back.

Always write yourself. Even if you are the leader, you are part of the group. And be prepared to read back, even if it is only a couple of lines.

When everyone's finished, ask them to go through their work and tidy their piece up. You may wish to move on at this stage (but ask if anyone's written anything extraordinary which they would like to share; limit to two people if necessary).

Alternatively, you can take the exercise further by inviting them to quarry their writing and turn it into a poem. That is, they write again, incorporating the free-writing – or else they edit and amend more thoroughly on the page. Some may feel their work is exactly right as it came out (these will be either brilliant or awful). You may have to talk about drafting.

The Bloody Machine Gun. A variant of the above. This uses five free-writing lines, given at intervals. From each they write for two minutes, after which you ask them to leave a space, then continue straight away with the next. When they've finished, they have to choose the one(s) they like best/dislike least and use it/them to start a poem.

Whispers. A follow up to the free-writing. Ask the group to underline one word, or if you prefer one line – not necessarily a sentence – that they like. They each read this out, once only, while the others write down what they think they've heard. From this each member will have a list of words or lines. They have then to write a poem including at least three (preferably more) of the key words or phrases.

*

HANDS. Read Ted Hughes's poem, 'Hands' from *Moortown*. Talk about the way the poem describes the whole person by concentrating on the hands; discuss the way the opening stanza contrasts with the last. Notice particularly how, when the farmer has gashed his hand on barbed wire, he 'flailed his hand like a caned boy': one short simile tells us as much as a stanza would about the farmer's schooldays. The workshop then makes notes about a friend or relative's hands, again trying to describe the whole person – and their personality – through the hands, and looking if they like for a simile that does a comparable job. Attention to nails, rings, jewellery, colour etc. The poem should open and close with what the hands are doing. A follow-up exercise could begin with a reading of Thom Gunn's 'The Feel of Hands' (*Selected Poems*).

VIEW FROM A WINDOW. The writers are in their bedroom/living room/kitchen. Have them imagine they are looking as far as they can to the right. Then to the left. They jot down everything they can see. Something happens outside. What is it? They write about it.

*

INTENSIVE WRITING. You ask a series of questions to which your group responds by writing – at once – a line or two lines of poetry for each. After a dozen questions they have the skeleton of a poem. The writers must be resourceful; sometimes you will ask questions they have incidentally already covered. Can be used in many ways – for instance writing the 'view from a window' as they go (instead of taking notes at their own pace). One that tends to work for me is:

The Living Room. Adapt the questions below to suit your approach. The group close their eyes and imagine they are in their hallway or kitchen. They are walking toward their living room. The living room door is closed. Have them imagine the feel of the door handle. They open the door:

– What is the first thing you see in the living room? Write a line or two lines about it.
– Where have you come from? Elaborate. Again, one or two lines.
– You go to sit in an armchair. There is a magazine beside it. Write a line or two lines about riffling through the pages, finding an interesting article.
– What is the line that stands out (perhaps a headline). Write it down verbatim.
– What time of day is it, and what does this mean (e.g. someone will soon be home from work). A line or two lines.
– You look round the room. Notice an object which is always there but which you rarely look at. What is it? What does it remind you of (either a simile or the associations the object has). Line or two lines.
– What can you hear? May not necessarily be in the room (perhaps next door/outside). And what does it sound like (simile)? Line or two lines.

– Look round the room again. There's something there which ties in – somehow – with either the magazine article or the sound (or both). Write a line or two lines.

– You go over to the window (write this briefly). What do you see?

– Someone enters (or perhaps was already there). This person also comes over to the window, and comments on something outside. Line or two lines.

– Your reply, or what happens next. You have up to five lines to finish the poem.

You see how this might be adapted. Different situation, similar questions. The person who comes in might be carrying something: what is it, what does it signify? Other scenarios may be an attic, a bus stop, a railway station, a train journey…

Intensive writing can also be used with:

Postcards. Preferably "art" cards, but any will do; handed out, one each. The writers are trying to write a poem as they go along – one that will work without the card; they are not trying to answer the questions "correctly".

– What is the first detail you notice? Elaborate. A line or two lines.

– What time of day is it, and what does this mean?

– What is/are the main colour(s) in the card. What does it make you think of? A line or two lines in response.

– What do you hear in the card? What does it sound like (simile)?

– What is happening in the card? And why?

– There is a detail in the card you haven't noticed till now. Write a line or two about it.

– Write a line that follows from the last but including the word 'always'.

– If the painter/photographer had moved a fraction to the right, what would also be included in the scene? (What is happening just out of frame on the right?)

– Bring someone (yourself? a friend?) into the poem in some way.

– You have a maximum of five lines to finish the poem. Try to repeat a word or phrase from somewhere near the beginning of the poem. You *may* wish to end on a rhyme or half-rhyme.

Note that your poem needn't be about a specific painting – and needn't even mention art at all: there have been *a lot* of painting poems in the past few years. Because he is one of my favourite poets and because I hope you will search his work out, I will quote a 'painting' poem here by Stanley Cook (from his Littlewood Press *Selected Poems*):

Picture of a Cornfield

I stop, whatever exhibition is on,
Before this part of the permanent collection,
Wind it a little and shake it like a watch
Beyond repair that for a moment goes again.
This is the path the farmer ploughed up
When he sowed the corn, making a fool
Of the signpost showing a right of way,
Short-cut to the station people have trodden back.
Now at a distance their heads bob about
Among the ripened, rustling, foaming ears;
The miracle they made themselves stops them drowning.
The sky is blue and the trees are fully dressed
In dusty dark green leaves; wild pansies
Show their faces between the stalks of corn
And a rabbit panics out of a hedge.
People I know approach along the path
And almost reach the point where its beaten soil,
Like a trick explained, emerges from the field.
Before they speak, the walls of the gallery
Fade in again, as either the pull of the city
Asserts itself or I draw back in self-defence,
Finding as usual nothing to fit the question
How came I and the painter, whose dates are all
I know of him, in the same field in a different field
At the same time at a different time,
Feeling the same? Was everyone once there?

Postcard or picture sequence. A number of cards or photographs
– not necessarily connected – given to each person, who then has
to write about them in such a way as to establish a narrative. This
is a useful exercise for discussing the different freedoms (and constraints) in poetry and fiction and, of course, narrative technique
in general.

Guided Fantasy. Exactly as intensive writing, except you take
the group on an adventure. With some of these games, you might
want to *suggest* the group try imposing a pattern as they go along
– e.g. three lines stanzas – or, as they get more experienced, half-
rhyme for instance. This exercise though particularly lends itself

to a roughened blank verse. Make it clear before they begin that they will probably do a lot of writing.

– You are woken in the middle of the night. Your room is dark. You lie still, trying to identify why you woke. It is quiet.
– What can you hear?
– Turn your head to the right. There is a door, dimly glowing, where there never was a door before. You know you shouldn't, but you get out of bed to investigate. Write about this.
– What is the door like? Describe it. Describe opening it.
– There are steep steps the other side. You go down them. What is it like? You are barefoot: describe the steps – cold? carpeted? slimy?
– The stairs are half-lit: light source?
– Something goes past you, disappears. What is it? How do you feel?
– The stairs open into a hallway. Describe it. Describe your walking forward.
– What can you hear? What is it like (simile)?
– What can you smell? What is it like (simile)?
– You enter a larger hall. There are paintings on the walls. What are they of? How do you feel about them?
– You hear something which makes you leave at once. What is it? You cannot find the stairs, only a door. You struggle with the door. Open it:
– What is the first thing you see?
– What happens next/What is in the room?
– There is also a casket or chest. What is in it?
– Now there is a person in the room. Who is it? What do they say to you?
– What happens next? (You can't return to your bedroom; it can't 'all have been a dream'.)

It may be that they have the start of a narrative poem or short story, or, perhaps more likely, that one section of the piece may be worth focussing on to make a separate poem.

Similar guided fantasies – make up your own linkage – include a walk through a forest: you come to a house in a clearing, enter it. Or a walk along a seashore or lakeside. You walk into the water, go on walking. You can breathe water. You see a light, swim towards it: a sunken ship/an underwater city. Questions to begin an investigation.

Having people go down those stairs, or into a wood or underwater, registers that they are entering the subconscious. Choose your questions and guide-material carefully, tailor it to your group. Invent your own scenario.

*

The Mystery Object. Place a box on the table. The group has to write down what they think is in it, and then, at speed and any way they like, they have to write about it. After a few minutes, ask them to stop and close their eyes.

You then take out the mystery object: anything at all: an orange, a book, a paintbrush, a shoe. They open their eyes and again begin writing as fast as they can. An alternative is to have them keep their eyes closed and then hand them objects to feel and think about. Have two or three circulating round the group. You remove the objects without them opening their eyes. Then they begin writing.

The Suitcase. The group imagines finding a suitcase in an attic. How do they feel, finding it? Do they open it at once? What is in it? They write, as quickly and freely as they can.

Dramatic Monologues. These are often extremely effective, especially with new writers, because they can release a writer, the way that working with a mask does in drama. Here are some ideas:

Occupations: everyone is given a different job – plumber, undertaker, deep-sea diver, whatever; they then write a poem from their new perspective. Carol Ann Duffy's poem 'Warming Her Pearls' (see page 47) is a good example for the group to look at first.

Objects: everyone is given an object to speak in the voice of: a table, a telephone, a roll of wallpaper, whatever. See Sylvia Plath's poem 'Mirror'. This next poem, by Peter Sansom, has an object in a more specific context:

A stone in a drystone wall

I have lived so long in this wall
I might have been born here. My family
sit round me, hold me in, hold me up,
fallen once, built back.
At night the cold and often the rain.
I can feel it, it is not pure.

74

Part of me is gone, worn away
for the sake of a boundary,
for the sake of keeping one man's sheep
from another man's grass: little more
than scrubland that after all
would be stronger for cropping.

It is still night. I am aware of the stars
as I am of the seasons, though only for a moment
over the line of forest from my crammed-in
angle do I ever see a star.
I cannot imagine which constellation it belongs to.
It is dimmed and flickers
but never quite disappears.
Mostly I remember a time there was daylight,
the sun coming up like a promise honoured
and being warmed by it.

Invent your own contexts, but some of my favourites are

A vacuum cleaner in a shop window
A loose button on an old overcoat
A stained glass window in a derelict church
A lift in an office block
A motorbike in pieces on a kitchen floor
A wardrobe in a hotel bedroom
A spoon in a bedsitter
A bus shelter at midnight
A piece in a jigsaw of a landscape with scattered houses
A pub (P.H.) legend on an Ordnance Survey map
A bottle of aspirin in a bathroom cabinet
A safety match in a box in a cardigan pocket
A reading lamp on a tidy desk
A reading lamp on a cluttered desk
A roller blind at a window overlooking the sea
A paintbrush in a jar of turps

Baudelaire's Pipe. Write a poem from the point of view of e.g. John McEnroe's tennis racquet; Beethoven's piano; Philip Larkin's glasses ('The more he read / the thicker I got'), etc. You might look at Oliver Reynolds's poem, 'Baudelaire's Pipe' first (from his book *The Player Queen's Wife*).

All three of these can be 'games' if the writers keep their personae secret and the rest of the group try and guess the occupation/object.

Secret Poem: Members' poems handed in and passed round anonymously: group has to guess who wrote which. At least one person should counterfeit another's style.

Prose into poem. Newspaper article/history text/car manual photocopied and handed round for people to turn into poetry. A doddle.

Poem as Journal Entry (by someone from history/character in a book, film etc).

The Epigraph. Many poems have epigraphs, often in Greek. Ian McMillan has a poem called 'Loose', about a man who is not in any way a seahorse. McMillan decided to have an Arab proverb as epigraph. Not knowing any, he made one up: 'I offered myself a tent, but I did not accept it'. Make up a similarly inappropriate epigraph for a poem. Then write the poem.

The Furniture Game. This is a variant of the one given in Sandy Brownjohn's *Does It Have To Rhyme?* It lends itself to working in pairs or groups of four. Each team thinks of a famous person, someone everybody in the room will know. They keep it secret from the other teams. Then they write about this person in terms of the following categories: furniture; weather; car; drink; food; time; place; animal; book; film; flower; room etc.

If their person *were* a piece of furniture, what would it be? For instance, the Queen might be: 'A stiffbacked ornate chair in a mansion'. For 'weather' she would of course be 'raining'. Note that you're not asked what car she would *travel in* but what car she would actually *be*. Note also that for each category the groups have to write at least a line of poetry: one word is not enough. When the poems are finished a group leader is chosen to read each one out and the other groups must guess the famous person.

Forms. Using any of the above techniques, or a poem as starting point, have them write in a given form – e.g. quatrains/rhyming quatrains/half-rhyming quatrains; a sonnet, a villanelle etc. A sestina is interesting: you might supply most (or all) of the end words (choose these with care – see 'Sestina' in the section on given forms).

End words. Give the end-words of a (published) poem. You might include at least one blank (so they can have any word they like here). They have to fill in the rest of the poem.

Similarly, choose key words from *within* separate lines of a poem. Lay these words out on a blackboard (or large piece of card) roughly in the pattern of the original – i.e. one word in the middle of the first line; one word near the beginning of the second; towards the end of the third, etc. A tortuous follow-up would be to have them go through their poems changing the given words.

Beginning line/end line. Give the first and last lines of a poem. The group have to write the piece inbetween.

Music. Make a tape of contrasting pieces of instrumental music. Ask questions in the intensive writing format ('What is happening now?'; 'what can you see?'). Before writing begins it may be worth establishing a context which suits the music (e.g. crossing a desert; a walk across town at night; a space flight).

Sound effects. Make a tape from sound effect records (your library will stock them, complete with printed warning about infringement of copyright). Your tape should loosely tell a story – e.g. footsteps across gravel, a churchbell tolling; a gate opening. Release the sound effects singly (pause the tape for each intensive writing question) or else run the tape continuously and guide the writing as necessary.

What I Know *or* **What Is Worth Knowing.** I left this game till last because it gives me the chance to quote a genuine 'workshop' poem. Written in a group and derived as it was from another poem, it is nevertheless very much its own piece. I like it very much and not only because it is based on a poem I like very much, 'What Is Worth Knowing' from Sujata Bhatt's first book, *Brunizem*. Bhatt's poem has been the model for many other good poems, including one by Selima Hill. This one was written by Joyce Woodward. In this game any 'open' question can be asked, which the poem repeatedly answers:

What I Know
(after Sujata Bhatt)

That Wednesday is the middle of the week.
That they might have found the crater of the meteor
which buried all the dinosaurs.

You need ammonia to keep marble white.
The dumb cannot speak.
You can clone from any living cell.
We break up our cells so that in seven years you have changed
      entirely
so now you could meet that cloned self of seven years ago
and need to be introduced. How firmly you would have
to turn your back not to know that person.
That it takes only five years to tip the seesaw of the climate
into an ice age.
The American Indians had civilisations which stretched from
      the Arctic
to the Antarctic; they are now seen as ineducable.
Camphor held tight in airless cupboards keeps silver
almost permanently bright.
Rosemary is for remembrance.
Six million Jews were murdered in World War II.
Hiroshima had not been bombed before.
That Tuesday isn't the beginning or the end of the week.
That peace is indivisible.
That one church sees abortion as a mortal sin.
Scientifically speaking a bumble bee can't fly.
We exhale CO_2. Trees inhale CO_2.
The American colonists killed two million Indians
to farm the empty west.
Once there was one continent from which the others split.
They said Malthus was wrong about population,
then the Green Revolution.
Now we just wait for the numbers of people to double and double.
That there is a small brown bird, the last of its species,
calling every spring for its mate.
That three-quarters of a million children die of preventable diseases.
That at our galaxy's edge black holes devour stars.
Marble doesn't grow on Yorkshire hillsides.
They call the white flowers Moonpennies.
That Doncaster will be by the sea at the turn of the century.
That Lithuania wants to be independent.
That you need to keep your grass short
if you want to be thought respectable.

METRE, RHYME, HALF-RHYME
AND FREE VERSE

Using form

In this section I want to talk about **Given** or **fixed forms** (such as the sonnet or villanelle). If you are worried about these – if you are worried about "form" – it is probably because of *metre*, an area which for many years didn't so much worry as terrify me. For one thing the names – iamb, trochee, dactyl and so on – are *Greek*. But the main problem is that what we try and reduce in classes to a single arithmetical task – the counting of stressed and unstressed syllables – is actually a number of processes going on at once, and all of them at least to some degree a matter of opinion.

I find it difficult to remember the names, though in fact of course you can use a metre without having to be able to name it, just as we can use English without having to know the parts of speech. Imagine being asked for a poem rhyming *aabba*, consisting of two amphibrach trimeters, two amphibrachic dimeter lines and then an amphibrachic trimeter with a redundant first syllable. As long as you know to pronounce Dublin's port as *Dun Leary*, you can do it in your head:

$$- \quad / \quad - \quad - \quad / \quad - \quad - \quad / \quad / \quad -$$
A writer | I knew from | Dun Laoghaire

$$- \quad / \quad - \quad - \quad / \quad - \quad - \quad / \quad -$$
(whose poems | were brilliant | in theory)

$$- \quad / \quad - \quad - \quad / \quad -$$
would count all | the stresses

$$- \quad / \quad - \quad - \quad / \quad -$$
which'd really | impress us

$$(-) \quad - \quad / \quad - \quad - \quad / \quad - \quad - \quad / \quad -$$
though his limericks | (this is one) | were dreary.

Imagine being asked for another aabba, but this time made of two anapaestic trimeters, two anapaestic dimeters and a final trimeter – ensuring that the first three lines begin with an iambic substitution and all of them to end with an hypermetric foot...Which is in fact how my limerick would more usually be scanned, since limericks tend to be considered as basically anapaestic. (An anaepaestic foot is one that has two unstressed syllables followed by a stressed syllable, as in the word 'in-ter-RUPT': all these terms are explained shortly.) So, conventionally scanned, it would run like this:

_ / _ _ / _ _ _ / (_)
A wri | ter I knew | from Dun Laoghai | re

_ / _ _ / _ _ _ / (_)
(whose po | ems were brill | iant in theo | ry)

_ / _ _ _ / (_)
would count | all the stres | ses

_ _ / _ _ _ / (_)
which'd real | ly impress | us

_ _ / _ _ _ / _ _ _ / (_)
though his lim | ericks (this is | one) were dreary.

What's more, you notice that we don't count syllables slavishly but as they are actually used in normal speech (though we do allow some metrical latitude). We don't hear three syllables in 'brilliant' ('bril-li-ant') for instance, or in 're-al-ly' or 'lim-er-icks', but more nearly 'bril-yant', 'rear-ly' and 'lim-ricks'.

I'm going to look a bit more at metre in a moment. You see already how scanning verse is quite a tricky matter of judgement. But let's not panic. After all we only have to *write* the poems. It's the others I feel sorry for, sorting out stresses in exam rooms under their breath.

Rhythm

Try reading a newspaper article aloud, and you see – or rather hear – that stresses occur naturally, and that those stresses fall into rhythms, even in prose, even in *The Sun*. Everything has rhythm: the seasons, the heartbeat and the sea are the more obvious examples. We like rhythm. When people say, 'for me if it doesn't rhyme…', they mean *rhythm* and rhyme. But only a certain kind: like a pendulum that's swinging, it's/the kind that keeps its beat.

As you get better at reading, at listening to poems, your ear becomes attuned to more subtle effects in which rhythm and meaning can marry more exactly, the rhythm working with the poem. An unsophisticated rhythm usually distorts or else *replaces* meaning.

Poetry's rhythm is more noticeable than prose's because in prose the rhythms constantly change; a poem is more limited, and more sharply defined, and its rhythm is set out in line units. If the lines are even more sharply defined, so that their stresses are falling into a fairly regular pattern, we call it metre. In other words, metre is rhythm that has been organised into a recognisable given pattern.

Prosody (pronounced with short Os) is the jargon for 'the science of versification': that is, dealing with metres and the practice of scansion. It has nothing to do with prose. **Scansion** is deciding which syllables carry stresses and which are unstressed, and finding a pattern in or patterns to the rhythms in the poem. Scansion is seeing how a poem scans. We are not looking for mathematical precision: what we're doing is translating stress-sounds into written notation. Some lines are difficult to scan until we can hear the *predominant* metre. Look again at my limerick for instance: that last line has an extra unstressed syllable (the 'though') and a swallowed syllable (the 'er' in 'limericks').

Descriptions not prescription

When we look at a poem and notice that it has fourteen iambic pentameter lines that rhyme *ababcdcdefefgg*, we may call it a Shakespearean sonnet. Stray too far from that scheme (fifteen lines for instance) and the poem ceases to be a Shakespearean sonnet, though it may still be a fine poem and one that comments on or in some way exploits our expectations of a Shakespearean sonnet.

All of the main fixed forms existed by the 16th century, so it's not surprising that over time some have come unfixed, or at least been wobbled about a bit – adapted, extended, truncated, made new. Part of the point of using a form is indeed that you are working within its tradition and being subject to its constraints; though of course that is only *part* of the point: *the* point is to create a living poem, not a waxworks dummy of the Earl of Surrey.

You should be aware that if you adapt a fixed form you are doing two things: you are fiddling about with a mechanism which has a proven track record – are you really *improving* the way it works by customising it? And also, of course, you are going to challenge reader expectations and invite comparisons.

Using metre

Metre also has an effect on the reader, as Coleridge points out:

As far as metre acts in and for itself, it tends to increase the vivacity and susceptibility both of the general feelings and of the attention. This effect it produces by the continued excitement of surprize and by the quick reciprocations of curiosity still gratified and re-excited, which are too slight indeed to be at any

81

one moment objects of distinct consciousness, yet become considerable in their aggregate influence. As a medicated atmosphere, or as a wine during animated conversation, they act powerfully, though themselves unnoticed.

Metre has its effect on the writer, too. 'I write in metre because I am about to use a language different to prose', as Coleridge also says. Though it's true that metre seems to get some writers steaming drunk, generally it doesn't just generate the poem, but can actually help order and discipline it. John Donne:

I thought if I could draw my pains
Through rhyme's vexation, I should them allay.
Grief brought to numbers cannot be so fierce,
For, he tames it, that fetters it in verse.

['The Triple Fool']

Coleridge has a proviso about metre, though: 'where, therefore, correspondent food and appropriate matter are not provided for the attention and feelings thus roused, there must needs be a disappointment felt; like that of leaping in the dark from the last step of a staircase, when we had prepared our muscles for a leap of three or four' [from *Biographia Literaria*].

We needn't worry about metre, as long as it sounds natural – that is, appropriate. All that metre does, of course, is establish a pattern. And not for its own sake, but so that (together with other sonic devices) the poem can marry the sound of its words to their thought and feeling. A striking example of this is in the poem 'Wind' where Ted Hughes introduces – against a predominantly iambic flow – a series of stressed monosyllables: 'a black/back gull bent like an iron bar slowly'. You have no option, reading that aloud, but to have the words put their back into it.

That rather sci-fi term 'sonic devices' means in this context only **alliteration** and **assonance**. The first is the repetition of consonants: 'black back gull bent like an iron bar slowly' (and also the 'k' sounds at the end of 'black' 'back and like'); the second is the repetition of vowel sounds: 'black back' and 'like an iron'. There is modulation too in 'slowly' which has a longer, slower vowel sound. These do make a difference of course to the way we read – and scan – and indeed *understand* the line.

Free verse

The point of **free verse** of course is that it *doesn't* have the constraints of fixed form poetry, and that the reader has no formal expectations. Or not quite. As Eliot noted in 1917, around the time of its inception, 'the most interesting verse which has yet been written in our language has been done either by taking a very simple verse form, like the iambic pentameter, and constantly withdrawing from it, or taking no form at all, and constantly approximating to a very simple one' ['Reflections on Vers Libre'].

Writing free verse is "easier" than using a fixed form, in that it takes less effort to write bad free verse than a bad villanelle. Free verse uses none of the established metrical patterns nor, strictly speaking, of rhyme and stanza. Instead it relies on other devices such as alliteration and assonance and the way words are laid out on the page; and though it doesn't have a metre it often establishes patterns in rhythms through the repetition of words and grammatical structures.

Nevertheless, ultimately, some poems are poems only because we call them poems (especially prose poems). Look at William Carlos Williams's poem again on page 38. What is it that makes that a poem? Because it is called a poem, we read it differently than we would read, say, a paragraph in a newspaper: we read it with more attention, alert and open to verbal texture, the pauses effected by line and stanza break, the patterns of sound, image and idea; and we bring to our reading what we know about other poems it resembles or is in reaction against. It was written as a poem: it is read as a poem: therefore it is a poem. Though of course not necessarily a good poem.

Equally, there are metrically sound, rhyming pieces, which are not intended as poems but as adverts, say, or greeting card verse.

Eliot talked about vers liberé, free̲d verse. To make it clear that *free verse* has structure and organising principle, some Americans prefer the term *open-form*.

Metre

There are four main kinds:
   1) Strong stress metre
   2) Syllabic metre
   3) Quantitative metre and
   4) Accentual or syllabic stress metre.

Only the fourth need concern us, generally speaking. But I'll explain a little about the others.

1. Strong stress metre. This is one of the earliest metres. In the 14th century William Langland was using it for his *Piers Plowman*, whose prologue opens:

In a sómer séason – when sóft was the sónne,

I shópe me in shróudes – as a shép wére,

In hábite as an héremite – unhóly of wérkes

Went wýlde in this wórlde – on Málvern húlles

Strong stress is easy to scan because it regards only the important "sense" words. Lines vary freely in their number of syllables; the operative patterning coming from the four stresses – two in each half of the line – and from the alliteration. G.S. Fraser points out that children often use this metre when writing poems: getting four stresses in among a lot of redundant, unstressed syllables. He notes too that all iambic pentameter lines can *also* be scanned as strong stress metre.

Strong stress metre fell out of favour even during the medieval period. Indeed Chaucer, almost contemporaneously with Langland, was writing a more flexible and subtly alliterative verse, influenced by his continental travels. Yet it's true that a number of later writers have had recourse to it; not least for instance Coleridge (*Christabel*) and W.H. Auden ('Reader to Rider').

2. Syllabics. If you are pushed this is French, really. French is a mainly unaccented language. As long as he has rudimentary arithmetic, even a man with a tin ear can manage this one, because all you do is count syllables (not stresses). Haikus are syllabic, of course. But syllabics can have any pattern you like. A poem about a pyramid for instance might have one syllable in the first line, two in the second, three in the third and so on...

Thom Gunn, among others, has written to good effect in syllabics. To my mind, though, syllabics are more useful to the poet or workshop leader than the reader. It gives the poet (and teacher) something fairly easy to work with and against – but we cannot hear syllabics (unless, which is often the case, the syllables actually approximate to a metrical pattern). Which is to say, do not clip or pad out your lines to suit a form which the reader gets no compensating benefits from.

3. Quantitative metre. If you are Greek or Roman and living in 68 BC, this one's for you. It works by measuring how long it takes to pronounce a stressed (long) or unstressed (short) syllable. 'Bit' for instance is shorter than 'Bid' is shorter than 'Bide'. Spenser, Coleridge, Tennyson and Bridges have used quantitative metre; and in practice I think many poets are – consciously or otherwise – aware of the patterns of long and short syllables in their (for instance) iambic pentameter lines.

4. Accentual or syllabic stress. This is the one you must know. This regards both accented (stressed) and unaccented (unstressed) syllables in a line. It is the most common system of measurement in English metrics.

Groups of syllables are jobbed together under the name *foot*. For instance:

I wan I dered lone I ly as I a cloud

The feet are demarked by the strokes. Notice that feet disregard sense and often break in the middle of a word ('I wan |' is the first foot). This line is an iambic tetrameter; that is, it has four iambic feet.

The iamb is a two-syllable foot (the first syllable unstressed, the second stressed). We read the line

_ / _ / _ / _ /
I wan I dered lone I ly as I a cloud

Spoken English approximates naturally to iambic rhythm, which is why it is the most common metre in our poetry. There are many different kinds of feet, though I would guess iambic pentameter (five iambic feet: pent = 5) is the most common. Unrhymed iambic pentameter is called **blank verse** (as distinct from the non-metrical **free verse**). Much of Shakespeare, Wordsworth's *Prelude*; Milton's *Paradise Lost*, and literally thousands of other poems are in blank verse, including this – just over a quarter – from the middle of 'Birches' by Robert Frost:

One by one he subdued his father's trees
By riding them down over and over again
Until he took the stiffness out of them,
And not one but hung limp, not one was left
For him to conquer. He learned all there was
To learn about not launching out too soon
And so not carrying the tree away
Clear to the ground. He always kept his poise
To the top branches, climbing carefully
With the same pains you use to fill a cup
Up to the brim, and even above the brim.
Then he flung outward, feet first, with a swish,
Kicking his way down through the air to the ground.
So was I once myself a swinger of birches.
And so I dream of going back to be...

The last line quoted and perhaps lines 3, 6 and 7, are exact iambic
pentameter. There is a tricky bit in the middle of 7 where 'carrying' is elided – but you see how it is regular compared to line 8
with its opening inverted foot, which puts a stress on '<u>Clear</u> to | the
ground'... Note that though most of these have ten syllables, as
long as it has five stresses, a pentameter line can have nine or eleven
syllables.

Another popular form – it is the staple of 'Christmas card'
verse for instance – is **ballad metre**: iambic tetrameter alternating with trimeter as in Wordworth's

She lived | unknown, | and few | could know | [four feet]

When Lu | cy ceased | to be; | [three feet]

But she | is in | her grave, | and, oh, | [four feet]

The dif | ference | to me | [three feet]

Generally, depending on which sort of feet you are using (anapaest
is made up of three-syllable feet, for instance) lines go from the
rare monometer (one foot) through to an eight-foot (octameter)
line and beyond:

Monometer: one-foot line
dimeter: two-foot line
trimeter: three-foot line
tetrameter: four-foot line
pentameter: five-foot line
hexameter: six-foot line
heptameter: seven-foot line
octameter: eight-foot line.

Scanning a line of metrical poetry involves identifying the feet:

The iamb (iambic): invént

the trochee (trochaic): ónly

the anapaest (anapaestic): interrúpt

the amphibrach (amiphibrachic): arrángemènt

the dactyl (dactylic): ténderly

the spondee (spondaic): brów-béat

the pyrrhic: in a

Iambic *(Gray)*:

The cur | few tolls | the knell | of par | ting day

Trochaic *(Cook)*:

Large size | leather | leaves of | ivy | fall * (−)

---

* (*Above*) Incomplete or catalectic feet. Like a rest in music we hear the rhythm continue for the period of an unstressed syllable, continuing the sense of the line, though of course without words.

† (*Page 88*) An extra or hypermetric foot. Even simple nursery rhyme metre, you see, can be metrically quite sophisticated when it is scanned.

Anapaest *(Byron)*:

```
  –   – /  –   –    /   – –  /  –   –  /
The Assyr | ian came down | like the wolf | on the fold
  –   – / –    –    /    – – /   –  –  /
And his co | horts were gleam | ing in pur | ple and gold
  –    –    /     –  –    /   –   /    –   –   /
And the sheen | of their spears | was like stars | on the sea
  –   –   /   –    –    /   –  –  /    – – /
When the blue | wave rolls night | ly on deep | Galilee.
```

Amphibrachic *(Astley)*:

```
 –   /   –   – /  –  –  /   –  –   /   –
The place is | Islayev's | estate in | the country,
 –    /    –    –    /  –  –   /  –    –   /    –
this framework | his latest | construction: | 'That nonsense
  –     /   –   –   / –   –   /  –   –    /   –
will harness | the river, | and give him | the freedom
 –    /   –   –   /  –   –   /  –   –   /  –
to grow what | he wants. If | he's working | he's happy.
 –   /   –   –    /   –   –  /   –   – /  –
She turns to | me, languid. | His wife. And | the woman
  –    /   –   –   / –   – /  –  –  /  –
I've loved more | than any. | Natalya | Petrovna.
```

Dactylic:

```
 / – –  /  – –  /  ( – – )
Hickory, | dickory | dock †
```

Note that the next line, though, is iambic:

```
 –   /   –   /   –   /
The mouse | ran up | the clock
```

When the stress falls on the end syllable(s) of a foot, it is called a **rising** metre; when at the beginning, as in the trochee, it is called **falling**. You can see the different effects these have; the trochaic rhythm of Stanley Cook's line reinforces its sense. Similarly, the Byron passage with its headlong, breakneck anapaests.

The thing to remember is that (as in William Stafford's poem) you are quite at liberty to mix different sorts of feet. So long as your poem keeps predominantly to its metre – so that we can hear it underpinning the piece – you can afford considerable variation.

The opening feet, particularly in a mainly iambic line, often come **inverted** for some reason (and are then trochees). Which is why, incidentally, when you are scanning a line of verse, you should start from the end of it and work backwards. If you're having trouble scanning a line – particularly in your own poem – refer to **distributed** or **hovering stress**. That is, that although there are, say, four stresses as you'd expect in tetrameter, they are not always evenly spaced in their line. I should warn/reassure you that it is often impossible to identify a metre with any certainty – especially if you look at it long enough, which can be like repeating a word so often that it seems meaningless.

In any case, metre is not there for its own sake, and least of all for a reader to put squiggles over. It is in service of the poem. And it has to be working *with* the other devices – alliteration, assonance, rhyme, whatever – and of course with the meaning. As ever, I think that when you are using a metre properly, you are only partly conscious of handling it, and in practice, once you're experienced in it, the metre and its variations will by and large look after themselves.

It's worth remembering at this point I.A. Richards's 'dummy poem'. This was one that copied the *aural* qualities in another poem (which a group had already analysed). The 'dummy' had similar patterns of assonance, consonance and alliteration, and similar end rhyme and metre as the original poem, and yet, because of course it *meant* something different (since it used different words), the dummy did not reproduce the emotive effects of the original.

Rhyme

Like metre, rhyme is a way of creating sound patterns. You can hear a rhyme any time, though it rarely shows in everyday prose, since that does not have a metre to make it sound completer. Also because of course the prose-writer is not *expected* to use rhyme, and therefore the reader does not expect to hear it.

Rhymes that use single syllable words ('man/plan') or words with a final stressed syllable, such as 'command/unplanned', are called **masculine rhyme**. **Feminine rhyme** is a rhymed stressed syllable followed by one or more rhymed unstressed syllables, as in 'water/slaughter' or 'watering/slaughtering'.

Internal rhyme puts at least one of the rhymes inside the line – 'it might rhyme at any time', though you may need to be careful with this because, necessarily coming close together, such rhymes can seem jingly. The more usual sort – **end rhyme** – are equally jingly of course if the lines are short, and if you are using **full-rhyme** ('honk' and 'conk'). In full-rhymed poems you sometimes get **eye rhymes**, which only look as if they rhyme –'brow' and 'glow' for instance; though in fact you could say that 'brow' and 'glow' are **half-** or **near-rhyme**. As are 'cat' and 'pet', the end consonants having the same sound; and 'cat' and 'bag' where the vowels have the same sound.

Strictly speaking repetition is not rhyme, though you could say it has the same effect as full-rhyme, only more so; as in this from Paul Muldoon's 'History': 'And into the room where MacNeice wrote 'Snow', / Or the room where they say he wrote 'Snow'.' **Rime riche** uses homophones: words that sound exactly the same but have different spellings and meanings: 'hear/here'; 'sight/site'.

My feeling is that half- or near-rhyme is generally a more subtle and pleasing device than full-rhyme. It also affords you more scope of course: consider how predictable full-rhymes might have been with that cat. Or think for a moment about an 'orange' and its possible rhymes. Near-rhyme allows you not just such words as 'strange' or 'porridge' but could even if you are daring introduce *Boris*. Look again at the occasional half-rhymes in 'November' (page 44). You see that if they fall with the stresses, they can fall with some effect.

EIGHT

SOME GIVEN FORMS

Stanzas

Poems are generally arranged in verses, or, as we tend to say now, **stanzas**. (A 'verse' usually appears in a *rhymed* poem; though it is ambiguous in that poems are sometimes called 'verses', and poetry itself 'verse'. It can also mean 'light verse' or birthday-card poetry.) 'Stanza' – which is Italian for 'room' – is the equivalent of a paragraph in prose. There are individual terms for some stanzas: one of four lines is called a quatrain, for instance.

line: a line
couplet: two lines
tercet : three lines
quatrain: four lines
quintain or quintet: five lines
sestet: six lines
septet: seven lines
octave: eight lines

Some stanza and given forms

Lots to choose from. But the simplest is the rhyming quatrain (four line stanza). We mark the rhymes with letters.

Because I could not stop for Death –	(x)
He kindly stopped for me –	(a)
The Carriage held but just Ourselves –	(x)
And Immortality.	(a)

Non-rhyming lines, as you see, we call 'x'. In the opening to this Emily Dickinson poem, you see the form is uncomplicated – only one rhyme to find and an easy metre: iambic lines interlacing tetrameter (four feet) with trimeter (three feet). The tone and diction are colloquial, in fact chatty. It continues:

We slowly drove – He knew no haste
And I had put away
My labor and my leisure too,
For His Civility –

We passed the School, where Children strove
At Recess – in the Ring –
We passed the Fields of Gazing Grain –
We passed the Setting Sun –

Or rather – He passed Us –
The Dews drew quivering and chill –
For only Gossamer, my Gown-
My Tippet – only Tulle –

We paused before a House that seemed
A Swelling in the Ground –
The Roof was scarcely visible –
The Cornice – in the Ground –

Since then – tis Centuries – and yet
Feels shorter than the Day
I first surmised the Horses' Heads
Were toward Eternity –

('Tippet' is an overscarf, apparently, and 'tulle' is stiffened gauze.)
This was written in the middle 1800s – hence the capitalised nouns;
so it may seem that the rhymes are surprisingly free, apart from
that repetition 'Ground/Ground'. (Not half- but one-hundredth
rhyme that 'Ring/Sun'!) Yet they don't sound free because of the
strong, definite metre. And also, to an extent, because the 'rhyme'
words accord with each other: 'the day' balances with 'Eternity'
'stopped for me' contrasts with 'immortality'; and even the notion
of a setting sun draws meaning from (closed but eternal) 'the
ring'. Rhyme is not, as I said earlier, just there for binding; the
rhyme words have to have some semantic relation to each other
too.

The next one really *is* chatty, since it was 'Overheard in County
Sligo': the first two lines were the starting point for the poem. It is
ballad metre (four stresses alternating with three) and again only
the second and fourth lines rhyme.

I married a man from County Roscommon
And I live at the back of beyond
with a field of cows and a yard of hens
and six white geese on the pond.

92

At my door's a square of yellow corn
caught up by its corners and shaken,
and the road runs down through the open gate
and freedom's there for the taking.

I had thought to work on the Abbey stage
or have my name in a book,
to see my thought on the printed page,
or still the crowd with a look.

But I turn to fold the breakfast cloth
and to polish the lustre and brass,
to order and dust the tumbled rooms
and find my face in the glass.

I ought to feel I'm a happy woman
for I lie in the lap of the land,
and I married a man from County Roscommon
and I live in the back of beyond.

GILLIAN CLARKE

The next is a **closed quatrain** – that is, the middle rhymes are
sandwiched by the outer ones.

Much have I travell'd in the realms of gold,	(a)
And many goodly states and kingdoms seen;	(b)
Round many western islands have I been	(b)
Which bards in fealty to Apollo hold.	(a)

Keats. Tricky to scan the first line, but it is clearly iambic pentameter. Remember it's easier to scan back from the end of the
lines, since these often have inverted feet to kick off with.

   Of course there's more to the poem:

Oft of one wide expanse had I been told	(a)
That deep-brow'd Homer ruled as his demesne;	(b)
Yet did I never breathe its pure serene	(b)
Till I heard Chapman speak out loud and bold:	(a)

These two quatrains are run together (i.e. no stanza break) and form
the **octave**. The last six lines have no stanza break either:

Then felt I like some watcher of the skies (c)
 When a new planet swims into his ken; (d)
Or like stout Cortez when with eagle eyes (c)
 He stared at the Pacific – and all his men (d)
Look'd at each other with a wild surmise – (c)
 Silent, upon a peak in Darien. (d)

All sonnets are or at least approximate to iambic pentameter. One of the reasons for all the inversions is that Keats has only four rhyme sounds, distributed equally between the **octave** (first eight lines) and the **sestet** (last six). Traditionally there is a change of mood or movement after the octave; the rhyme underlining this: 'Then felt I like some watcher of the skies' comes as a surprise.

So. This sonnet is built of two closed quatrains (which nevertheless interlace: handy, since they develop the theme) with an alternate rhyming sestet. Moreover, the sestet, you can say, is actually two **tercets** (three line stanzas), the first of which gives an example of the theme, the second concluding the theme. You can tell it isn't a **Shakespearean sonnet** at a glance, because it doesn't end with a rhyming couplet. Less easy to tell it isn't **Miltonic**: both this and Milton's are based on the **Italian** or **Petrarchan** model. (Petrarchan isn't quite synonomous with Italian, but talk as if it is, nobody will argue.) Milton's, as it happens, break their sense later than the octave. Usually at the tenth or eleventh line. He tends not to **end-stop** his lines, but runs the sense on (**enjambement**), thereby tightening the poem's movement and helping disguise his rhymes. This last is worth bearing in mind. Many first solo runs in a sonnet plummet precisely because the rhymes are obvious, the lines each a unit of sense. Pause – with a comma, colon, semicolon or (why not go the whole hog?) even a full stop – mid line. That will break things up a bit. A mid-line break in rhythm is called a **caesura**.

Shakespeare, of course, was red-hot at sonnets. He was particularly good at those final couplets. The couplet is **epigrammatic**, summing up or commenting on the preceding twelve lines. He rhymes *ababcdcdefefgg*; in other words three quatrains, each themselves interlaced but distinct from each other, followed by the *gg*. So in the fourteen lines half are new rhymes: plenty more scope for us (English has few rhyme words compared to, say, Italian). And the separate quatrains give us the choice to blur theme and movement or not, as the sense requires.

The **Petrarchan** sonnet rhymes *abba, abba, cde cde*.

The **Spenserian** is *abab, bcbc, cdcd, ee*. Which is, to say the least, technically demanding.

Note that you needn't lump all your sonnet together. You can have stanza breaks after quatrains, or even, if you like, in odder patterns: leaving one line, for instance, on its own. Tony Harrison uses a sixteen-line sonnet, which is sometimes called a **tailed sonnet** or else a **Meredithian sonnet** (after the Victorian poet George Meredith, who used it for his *Modern Love* sequence). Harrison's poem you see is metrically regular and has full-rhymes, though it is laid out mainly in couplets:

Book Ends (1)

Baked the day she suddenly dropped dead,
we chew it slowly that last apple pie.

Shocked into sleeplessness you're scared of bed.
We never could talk much, and now don't try.

You're like book ends, the pair of you, she'd say,
Hog that grate, say nothing, sit, sleep, stare...

The 'scholar' me, you, worn out on poor pay,
only our silence made us seem a pair.

Not as good for staring in, blue gas,
too regular each bud, each yellow spike.

A night you need my company to pass
and she not here to tell us we're alike!

Your life's all shattered into smithereens.

Back in our silences and sullen looks,
for all the Scotch we drink, what 's still between 's
not the thirty or so years, but books, books, books.

There are also unrhymed sonnets and often quite quirky variants. Experiment is often necessary: it is hard to write effectively in the traditional sonnet form today. Appropriate diction is the thing. Don't be Shakespearean – or Keatsian, or Miltonic. Be yourself, as you are, today. And that means, incidentally, that you can avail yourself of half-rhyme and that hovering rhythm. People who habitually write free verse sometimes have trouble turning to metrical poetry (and the sonnet in particular), being unable to find the rhythm. Which is pretty much essential. Get it drumming in your mind first. *Tum-ti tum* it if need be to start with – so long as it doesn't *stay* tum-ti tum.

Sonnet sequences. Only for the brave. For the foolhardy there's the **sonnet redoublé**: fifteen sonnets in which the last line of each is the first line of the next. The last line of the fourteenth sonnet repeats the first line of the first. The icing on the cake is the fifteenth sonnet, which is made of all fourteen previous linking lines, *in order*. (Hint: write the fifteenth sonnet first.) I know two recent redoublés which are not only technical tour-de-forces, but which actually work as poems – Grevel Lindop's 'Patchwork' in *A Prismatic Toy* (Carcanet) and Robert Johnstone's 'Chelsea' in *Eden to Edenderry* (Blackstaff).

Seamus Heaney – whose own often quite loosely handled sonnets are also very worth learning from – has said that:

A sonnet for example isn't fourteen lines that rhyme; a sonnet is a system of muscles and enjambements and age and sex, and it's got a waist and a middle – it is a form...there are indeed fourteen lines and there are indeed rhyme words...but the actual movement of the stanza, the movement of the sonnet isn't there. I would like a distinction between form which is an act of living principle and shape which is discernible on the page, but inaudible, and kinetically, muscularly unavailable. Poetry is a muscular response also, I feel. If you read a Shakespearean sonnet, a beloved Shakespearean sonnet, it's a dance within yourself.

Michael Schmidt, whose *Reading Modern Poetry* this is quoted from, comments that Heaney's description is 'a timely corrective to the increasingly masonic 'new formalists' both in Britain and abroad who welcome a rhyme or a metrical stanza as a coded handshake and talk of *craft* as though the art of poetry were a kind of carpentry. It isn't. Skills are required, but skills, materials, tools, and a good work-bench do not ensure that the end product will be a poem.'

Finally on this, here are a pair of sonnets by David Constantine. Note the run-on lines and that extraordinary fifth line in the first: it is unusually long: the words 'Four days down' each take a stress and the rest of the line has five stresses on its own.

Lazarus to Christ

You are forgetting, I was indeed dead
Not comatose, not sleeping, and could no more
Wish for resurrection than what we are before
can wish for birth. I had already slid

Four days down when you hauled me back into the air.
Now they come to watch me break bread
And drink the wine, even the tactful plead
With dumb faces to be told something, and, dear,

Even you, who wept for me and of whom it is said
You know all things, what I mutter in nightmare
I believe you lie awake to overhear.
You too are curious, you too make me afraid

Of my own cold heart. However I wash
I cannot get the foist out of my flesh.

Christ to Lazarus

They faltered when we came there and I knew very well
They were already leaving me. Not one
Among your mourners had any stomach to go on,
And when they moved the stone and could smell

Death in his lair they slid off me like cloud
And left me shining cold on the open grave
Crying for you and heaving until death gave
And you were troubled in your mottled shroud.

They hid their eyes, they begged me let you stay,
But I was adamant, my friend. For soon
By a loving father fiercer than any moon
It will be done to me too, on the third day.

I hauled you out because I wanted to.
I never wept for anyone but you.

Another form enjoying a revival at the moment is the **villanelle**.
This recent one, by Derek Mahon, seems to me one of the real
triumphs of the form:

Antarctica

'I am just going out and may be some time.'
The others nod, pretend not to know.
At the heart of the ridiculous, the sublime.

He leaves them reading and begins to climb,
Goading his ghost into the howling snow;
He is just going outside and may be some time.

The tent recedes beneath its crust of rime
And frostbite is replaced by vertigo:
At the heart of the ridiculous, the sublime.

Need we consider it some sort of crime,
This numb self-sacrifice of the weakest? No,
He is just going outside and may be some time –

In fact, for ever. Solitary enzyme,
Though the night yield no glimmer there will glow,
At the heart of the ridiculous, the sublime.

He takes leave of the earthly pantomime
Quietly, knowing it is time to go.
'I am just going outside and may be some time.'
At the heart of the ridiculous, the sublime.

All villanelles are made of five tercets and a concluding quatrain. There are only two rhymes, the 'a's sandwiching the 'b's. The first and third lines are repeated, alternately, as the third line of subsequent stanzas throughout the poem until the final stanza, where the repeat lines become the final two lines of the poem. We give the repeat lines capital letters, and since they rhyme distinguish them by numbers:

A1bA2, abA1, abA2, abA1, abA2, and abA1A2.

The villanelle everyone thinks of is Dylan Thomas's 'Do not go gentle into that good night'. Duncan Curry's refers to Thomas in line thirteen of his own smaller-scaled piece:

All week I've laboured on a villanelle.	(A1)
I've mused and fretted and perspired	(b)
But I've not been doing very well.	(A2)

98

The rhymes are hard, the repeats are hell;	(a)
The whole scheme of things is rather tired.	(b)
All week I've laboured on a villanelle.	(A1)
I've a list of words from zel to hydrogel	(a)
But however I shuffle, it isn't inspired.	(b)
I've not been doing very well,	(A2)
For constantly the words rebel –	(a)
They fidget and won't line up as required.	(b)
All week I've laboured on a villanelle.	(A1)
Old D.T., good name for a lover of Bells,	(a)
could turn a mean villanelle – one to be admired –	(b)
But I've not been doing very well.	(A2)
Clearly it's a question of Hirondelle.	(a)
It must be whisky that has the desired –	(b)
All week I've laboured on a villanelle,	(A1)
And I've not been doing very well.	(A2)

You see both these villanelles are iambic pentameter, but there are some in iambic tetrameter – the shorter lines speeding up the movement to give the chiming rhymes and repeats more of a musical – or humorous – quality. I suppose the things to bear in mind when writing a villanelle are that the repeat lines must be well-chosen and that the tone and diction should stay appropriate all the way through. I saw a lot of villanelles when I worked for the *Orbis* Rhyme International competition. Most were so hung up on the idea of using a strict form that they sounded stilted and out-of-date. Only those that were contemporary and really *used* the circularity of the form had a chance of winning. Too often the form was an end in itself; or else traded in material that really needed to be cast in free or blank verse. With the possible exception of *Paradise Regained*, nothing is more boring than a middling villanelle.

I was forgetting. Middling **sestinas** are achingly tedious. They are nevertheless *in*. Sestinas don't as a matter of fact rhyme, though their strict use of repeat words makes them admissible in the aforementioned rhyme competition (the only reason some people write them).

What you have is six six-line stanzas (sestets) plus a three-line **envoi**, which rounds the poem off. The six end-words of the first stanza are all used as end-words in five other stanzas, in a changing pattern. So that it will work, you have to follow a formula where the end words shuffle round; beginning of course 123456 they then go to: 615243; 364125; 532614; 451362; 246531; plus the envoi using repeated words in the middle and ends of the lines as follows: 2 – 5; 4 – 3; 6 – 1.

For those like me with CSE maths, there is an easier way of looking at it. Say the end words of the *first* sestet are:

1 ———————————— thunder
2 ———————————— apartment
3 ———————————— country
4 ———————————— pleasant
5 ———————————— scratched
6 ———————————— spinach

Then the lines of the *second* sestet will end with the same words but in this order: last; first; next-to-last; next-to-first; next-to-next-to-last; next-to-next-to first. So the lines would end:

1 ———————————— spinach
2 ———————————— thunder
3 ———————————— scratched
4 ———————————— apartment
5 ———————————— pleasant
6 ———————————— country

This pattern (last; first etc) is used in the next sestet (country; spinach; pleasant; thunder; apartment; scratched) and with each of the other three sestets. Most sestinas are iambic, either tetrameter or pentameter. A celebrated example is Auden's 'Paysage Moralisé' ('Hearing of harvests rotting in the valleys'). I should point out that Neil Astley has two rather fine sestinas in his *Darwin Survivor* (Peterloo Poets), the second of which is in amphibrachic tetrameter (its opening stanza is quoted above in the 'Given Forms' section). But my next example doesn't have a regular metre at all. It is by John Ashbery and is called 'Farm Implements and Rutabagas in a Landscape':

The first of the undecoded messages read: 'Popeye sits in thunder,
Unthought of. From that shoebox of an apartment,
From livid curtain's hue, a tangram emerges: a country.'
Meanwhile the Sea Hag was relaxing on a green couch: 'How
          pleasant
To spend one's vacation *en la casa de Popeye*,' she scratched
Her cleft chin's solitary hair. She remembered spinach

And was going to ask Wimpy if he had bought any spinach.
'M'love,' he intercepted, 'the plains are decked out in thunder
Today, and it shall be as you wish.' He scratched
The part of his head under his hat. The apartment
Seemed to grow smaller. 'But what if no pleasant
Inspiration plunges us now to the stars? *For this is my country*.'

Suddenly they remembered how it was cheaper in the country.
Wimpy was thoughtfully cutting open a number 2 can of spinach
When the door opened and Swee'pea crept in. 'How pleasant!'
But Swee'pea looked morose. A note was pinned to his bib.
    'Thunder
And tears are unavailing,' it read. 'Henceforth shall Popeye's
    apartment
Be but remembered space, toxic or salubrious, whole or
    scratched.'

Olive came hurtling through the window; its geraniums scratched
Her long thigh. 'I have news!' she gasped. 'Popeye, forced as
    you know to flee the country
One musty, gusty evening, by the schemes of his wizened,
    duplicate father, jealous of the apartment
And all that it contains, myself and spinach
In particular, heaves bolts of loving thunder
At his own astonished becoming, rupturing the pleasant

Arpeggio of our years. No more shall pleasant
Rays of sun refresh your sense of growing old, nor the scratched
Tree-trunks and mossy foliage, only immaculate darkness and
    thunder.'
She grabbed Swee'pea. 'I'm taking the brat to the country.'
'But you can't do that – he hasn't even finished his spinach,'
Urged the Sea Hag, looking fearfully around at the apartment.

But Olive was already out of earshot. Now the apartment
Succumbed to a strange new hush. 'Actually it's quite pleasant
Here,' thought the Sea Hag. 'If this is all we need fear from
    spinach
Then I don't mind so much. Perhaps we could invite Alice the
    Goon over' – she scratched
One dug pensively – 'but Wimpy is such a country
Bumpkin, always burping like that.' Minute at first, the thunder

101

Soon filled the apartment. It was domestic thunder,
The color of spinach. Popeye chuckled and scratched
His balls: it sure was pleasant to spend a day in the country.

Obviously you have to be inventive with this one or you will soon
lose your reader. Sestina = siesta. Ashbery's tour-de-force gets a
lot of its energy from playing with the expectations of the form and
indeed with our expectations of the cartoon characters.

If you don't feel up to Ashbery, my tip is to choose end words
which have two or more meanings; and especially ones that can be
both verb and noun (for instance 'board'); and this is nicer still
when your words can be used as compounds, as in 'cupboard' and
turned then to 'all aboard', and even perhaps – though purists will
object – into 'all are bored'.

Ottava rima is eight lines of iambic pentameter rhyming *abababcc*.
'Ah yes,' you should say, 'the form credited to Boccaccio'. Keats
and others wrote in this form, though it was Byron's who exploited
its comic potential in his *Don Juan* and its prototype, 'Beppo':

But I am but a nameless sort of person
    (A broken Dandy lately on my travels),
And take for rhyme, to hook my rambling verse on,
    The first that Walker's Lexicon unravels,
And when I can't find that, I put a worse on,
    Not caring as I ought for critics' cavils;
I've half a mind to tumble down to prose
But verse is more in fashion, so here goes.

The **Spenserian** stanza is not always a barrel of laughs, but intelligently handled may well be a prizewinner. It is nine iambic lines,
eight of them pentameter and a concluding hexameter (call it an
alexandrine). It rhymes *ababbcbcc*. The interweaving rhyme gives
it a formal unity, and since the couplet is inexactly balanced – having
that extra foot – it doesn't necessarily effect closure. All this makes
it amenable to narrative. As in Spenser's allegorical verse-novel *The
Faerie Queen*; and in Keats's *Eve of St Agnes*:

Full on this casement shone the wintry moon,
And threw warm gules on Madeline's fair breast,
As down she knelt for heaven's grace and boon;
Rose-bloom fell on her hands, together prest,
And on her silver cross soft amethyst,
And her hair a glory, like a saint:

She seem'd a splendid angel, newly drest,
Save wings, for heaven: – Porphyro grew faint:
She knelt, so pure a thing, so free from mortal taint.

Anon his heart revives: her vespers done,
Of all its wreathed pearls her hair she frees;
Unclasps her warmed jewels one by one;
Loosens her fragrant boddice; by degrees
Her rich attire creeps rustling to her knees:
Half-hidden, like a mermaid in sea-weed,
Pensive awhile she dreams awake, and sees,
In fancy, fair St Agnes in her bed,
But dares not look behind, or all the charm is fled.

Not all of the poem is as sexy as this, the first voyeurism recorded in Spenserian stanzas; though this extract does give a glimpse of its sustained brilliance.

Another form which lends itself to the sequence or extended narrative is the **Pushkin stanza**, fourteen intricately-rhymed iambic tetrameters (or pentameters). Named after the author of the Russian masterpiece *Eugene Onegin*, the Pushkin stanza allows the writer to move freely through lyric, comic, dramatic and discursive moods. The best-known recent example is Vikram Seth's *The Golden Gate*. My quotation, though, is from Andrew Waterman's *Out for the Elements*, a poem which manages to stay readable through 178 verses. Its rhyme pattern is: *ababccddeffegg*.

6

Or take that teashop in South Norwood
where I once grew up, named 'The Horst
Café': every year more and more would
alter it with paint to read 'Worst
Café', and the man and his wife who
owned the place change it back, a life you
could hardly envy, soldiered through
repainting H on W.
Such can't be meant. Other dimensions
to their existences? No doubt.
But none improved what they slopped out
as tea. They've gone now, on their pensions
somewhere, paintbrush at last hung up,
crouched to the dregs of their last cup.

Terza rima. Terza rima is Italian for 'three rhyme', and is said to have been invented by Dante. It is generally iambic and has an interlocking rhyme scheme which is constantly moving forwards: *aba,bcb,cdc,ded* etc. This is by Carol Ann Duffy:

Terza Rima SW19

Over this Common a kestrel treads air	(a)
till the earth says *mouse* or *vole*. Far below	(b)
two lovers walking by the pond seem unaware.	(a)
She feeds the ducks. He wants her, tells her so	(b)
as she half-smiles and stands slightly apart.	(x)
He loves me, loves me not with each deft throw.	(b)
It could last a year, she thinks, possibly two	(c)
and then crumble like stale bread. The kestrel flies	(d)
across the sun as he swears his love is true	(c)
and, darling, forever. Suddenly the earth cries	(d)
Now and death drops from above like a stone.	(e)
A couple turn and see a strange bird rise.	(d)
Into the sky a kestrel climbs alone	(e)
and later she might write or he may phone.	(e)

The interest is sustained largely by the run-on lines and the italics, which slow and disturb the otherwise fluid movement you might expect in terza rima. Because it doesn't rhyme, 'apart' in line 5 is literally set apart; and is of course what the poem is all about. The closing couplet pulls the piece together, uniting the two strands that run through what is, we realise after all, a sonnet. One that needs more rhyme words than the traditional variety, and perhaps therefore manages more of a cumulative melody.

T.S. Eliot said something to the point here, that when he tried to imitate Dante, he was obliged to find a form which approximated to terza rima *without* rhyming. (The result is the air-raid passage in *Little Gidding*.) It is not just that English has fewer rhyme words than Italian, but that 'those which we have are in a way more emphatic.' I will quote the rest of the passage because it incidentally tells us something about the way rhyme works:

[English] rhyming words call too much attention to themselves: Italian is the one language known to me in which exact rhyme can always achieve its effect – and what the effect of rhyme is, is for the neurologist rather than the poet to investigate – without the risk of obtruding itself. I therefore adopted, for my purpose, a simple alternation of unrhymed masculine and feminine terminations, as the nearest way of giving the light effect of the rhyme in Italian. In saying this, I am not attempting to lay down a law, but merely explaining how I was directed in a particular situation. I think that rhymed *terza rima* is probably less unsatisfactory for translation of the Divine Comedy than is blank verse. For, unfortunately for this purpose, a different metre is a different mode of thought; it is a different kind of *punctuation*, for the emphases and the breath pauses do not come in the same place. Dante *thought* in *terza rima*, and a poem should be translated as nearly as possible in the same thought-form as the original. ['What Dante Means to Me']

Triolet. This is an eight line stanza which, like the villanelle, employs only two rhymes and two refrain lines: *ABaAabAB*. Hardy's 'At a Hasty Wedding' is one of the few real corkers I've come across:

If hours be years the twain are blest,	(A)
For now they solace swift desire	(B)
By bonds of every bond the best,	(a)
If hours be years. The twain are blest	(A)
Do eastern stars slope never west,	(a)
Nor pallid ashes follow fire:	(b)
If hours are years the twain are blest,	(A)
For now they solace swift desire.	(B)

Clever footwork in lines 3 and 4 keeps the poem on its toes.

The triolet is a cousin of the **Rondel**: two quatrains and a final quintet. The metre and rhyme are not fixed but the poem turns on two rhymes and two refrain lines. The first and second lines reappear as seven and eight, and the last repeats the first. I trust that is clear. *ABba, abAB,* and *abbaA.* You don't see many of these about, which is probably a very good thing.

The **Rondeau** is a variant of the Rondel, and therefore also related, on its mother's side, to the triolet. A Rondel can be up to fifteen lines, usually arranged in a quintet (*aabba*), a quatrain (*aabA*) and a sestet (*aabbaA*). Wyatt introduced it into English:

105

What no, perdy, ye may be sure!	(a)
Thinck not to make me to your lure	(a)
With wordes and chere so contrarieng,	(b)
Swete and sowre contrewaing;	(b)
To much it were still to endure.	(a)
Trouth is trayed where craft is in ure	(a)
But though ye have had my hertes cure,	(a)
Trow ye I dote withoute ending?	(b)
What no, perdye!	(A)

Though that with pain I do procure	(a)
For to forgett that ons was pure	(a)
Within my hert shall still that thing,	(b)
Unstable, unsure and wavering,	(b)
Be in my mynde withoute recure?	(a)
What no, perdye!	(A)

'Ure' in line 6 is no longer current; we would now say 'use', which would well and truly scupper the rhyme scheme. As with the triolet, villanelle, and all the 'rond' poems, the rondeau gives itself to musical effect, circularity of theme or subject and a modest euphony. It certainly needs to be heard aloud to be appreciated. This is even more true, I think, of

The **Roundel**, which was invented by its chief exponent, Swinburne. It is eleven lines in three stanzas, turning on two rhymes and a refrain: *RbaR*, *bab*, and *abaR*. The refrain is taken from the beginning of the first line and rhymes with lines two, five, seven and nine:

A roundel is wrought as a ring or a starbright sphere	(R/A)
With craft of delight and with cunning of sound unsought,	(b)
That the heart of the hearer may smile if to pleasure his ear	(a)
A roundel is wrought.	(R)

Its jewel of music is carven of all or of aught –	(b)
Love, laughter, or mourning – remembrance of rapture or fear	(a)
That fancy may fashion to hang in the ear of thought.	(b)

As a bird's quick song runs round, and the hearts in us hear	(a)
Pause answer to pause, and again the same strain caught,	(b)
So moves the device whence, round as a tear,	(a)
A roundel is wrought.	(R)

Masochists should be aware of the **rondeau redoublé**: five quatrains and a quintet with two alternating rhymes and five refrains based on the lines of the first stanza. The first half of line one is repeated in line 25; the whole first line reappears as line eight; line three as line 16; and line four as line 20. In other words, a piece of cake. I have not come across an example I like, but no doubt the above précis will suffice...

The **Pantoum** is increasingly popular as a workshop exercise, infrequently occasioning actually quite good poems. It is a Malay form, which the French and English imitated, no one is sure why. The Malayans had it as a quatrain in which the second couplet contained the meaning and the first couplet was a loosely related simile. Not a bad idea for a teaching session, in fact. But over here the pantoum is more nearly a villanelle, using repeat lines. It is generally twelve lines, in three quatrains. Lines 2 and 4 of the first stanza reappear as lines 1 and 3 of the second stanza and sometimes lines two and four of the last stanza are the same as lines one and three of the first.

Since it is achieved over six quatrains, it's tempting to call Mabel Ferrett's poem a pair of pantoums. You see how the repeat lines click into place and the final stanza returns us to the opening. And you hear that it is iambic trimeter (three stresses) with occasional dimeters (two stresses).

Rising Sap

After all earth is dead,	(A1)
all lovely things undone,	(B1)
a crocus rears its head,	(A2)
gold to the sun.	(B2)
All lovely things undone	(B1)
until a shaping force	(C1)
– gold to the sun –	(B2)
re-aligns its course;	(C2)
until a shaping force	(C1)
I feel, but cannot know,	(D1)
re-aligns its course	(C2)
as dry roots grow	(D2)

I feel, but cannot know,	(D1)
how in the end all things	(E1)
as dry roots grow	(D1)
burst into blossomings;	(E2)
how in the end all things	(E1)
with effortless delight	(F1)
burst into blossomings,	(E2)
dazzling the sight.	(F2)
With effortless delight	(F1)
after all earth is dead,	(A1)
dazzling the sight,	(F2)
A crocus rears its head.	(A2)

Haiku. The ultimate beginner's classroom poem: haikus help you to talk about imagery, concision and mood; and they have a fixed form which on the one hand gives the writer something to work within, but on the other is purely syllabic and so threatens no tantrums over metre. Only if you are Japanese or bananas should you call them either 'haikai' or 'hokku'. Haikus are lines of five, seven and five syllables respectively. Strictly, their imagery should be drawn from nature and you are meant to at least allude to one of the seasons; but since these measure gale force on the tedium scale, don't bother. Nobody does that anymore. Few people, indeed, write haikus. Few people, that is, except the coach-loads who turn up at writing weekends with folders full of the things. Try not to be one of these people, but if that's impossible, claim to be continuing the **imagist** tradition. Apparently, haikus are extremely demanding in Japanese, because putting words together in that language changes the meaning of *both* the words, and indeed of other words in their proximity. English of course doesn't work like that, which is perhaps why most English haikus stay what they are, very short, rather thin poems. My favourite is by John Cooper Clarke and goes something like:

Getting everything
in seventeen syllables
is very diffic

All the worse for being rarer at poetry events are the **Tanka** crew: these are usually smug, prematurely middle-aged men who consider themselves true craftspersons. The tanka is also called 'waka' and 'uta', names which I believe derive from the sound made by the legs of thick corduroy jeans as the poet struts up and down counting. Tankas are five lines of 5,7,5,7,7,7 syllables. Their theme is supposed to centre on love, nature, loss, that sort of thing. There is no double form called the **supertanka**. Until, that is, you invent it. Or any equivalent, e.g:

The **Torrey Canyon**. A tanka manqué: syllables as 5,7,5,7,1,1. Less formal in diction than the traditional tanka, but considerably more slick.

NINE

SOME POETS AND POEMS

Some Poets and Poems

And only *some*. There are many other poets I might and no doubt should have chosen. Still, there are plenty here, and my list is not a pantheon, but simply poets that I happen to have found new writers enjoy and can learn from. At the back of Paul Hyland's *Getting Into Poetry* (Bloodaxe) there is a heftier list, which includes a number of anthologies: these seem to me the place to start, then following up on individual authors who appeal to you.

I should say I'm not recommending modern writers instead of, say, Donne, Wordsworth, Keats, Browning, Yeats. It is of course just as important – in a sense more important – to really get to know the older poets as it is modern ones. Anthologies such as *The Penguin Book of English Verse* (Hayward) and the *Oxford Books* of various centuries will give you pointers. *The Norton Introduction to Poetry* (Hunter) is an ideal general anthology in its breadth and user-friendliness; it has excellent notes and clear sections explaining 'The Elements of Poetry'. Its cousin, *The Norton Anthology of Poetry* (Allison and others) is a more robust, detailed and comprehensive volume, ranging chronologically from medieval poetry through to the present day; again, it has good footnotes and a section on 'versification'.

Anthologies of more recent work include: *The Faber Book of Modern Verse* (ed. Roberts, revised Porter); the Penguins *New Poetry* (Alvarez), and *Contemporary American Poetry* (Hall). *The Penguin Book of Contemporary British Poetry* (Morrison and Motion) is good and easily come by, though I prefer the Carcanet alternative, *Some Contemporary Poets* (Schmidt). *The New Poetry* (Hulse, Kennedy, Morley: Bloodaxe) contains many engaging poets writing in the 80s and 90s. Similarly, *Poetry with an Edge* (Astley: Bloodaxe) is almost startling in the way it shows contemporary poetry as varied, exciting and alive. Bloodaxe also publishes *Hinterland: Caribbean Poetry from the West Indies and Britain* (Markham) and the remarkable *Sixty Women Poets* (France). I like *Ten Twentieth Century Indian Poets* (Parthasarathy: Oxford), and the *New Oxford Books of* – e.g. – *Canadian Verse* (Atwood) and *Australian Verse* (Murray). *The Faber Book of Contemporary American Poetry* (Vendler) and the Penguin *American Poetry* (Moore) are essential, I think, too. But you might start with George MacBeth's excellent *Poetry 1900 to 1975* (Longman). Well, already this is becoming unwieldy. Bear in mind that, if they haven't got them in stock, libraries can get hold of books for you.

Like its compiler, this list is fairly conservative. But the middle-ground is as good as any to work away from.

Robert Frost (1874-1963), *Selected Poems* (Penguin). Poems you might start with are: 'The Census Taker'; 'Stopping By Woods On A Snowy Evening'; 'Birches'; 'Mending Wall' and 'Out, Out –'. Frost's speciality is the colloquial but resonant line (Ian Hamilton points out that Frost often finds ordinary turns of phrase that are regular iambic pentameter). There is much to learn from Frost's handling of narrative and tone and from his selection and juxtaposition of detail; his best work is often near but not explicit allegory.

Edward Thomas (1878-1917), *Collected Poems*. Any edition will do, but the Oxford has excellent notes and previously unpublished work. Penguin do a *Selected Poems and Prose* which is very worth getting too. You might start with 'The Barn', 'Adlestrop', 'The Owl' and 'Old Man'. Thomas's pastoral Englishness (his parents were Welsh) is misleading. For instance, notice that 'Old Man' is, among other things, about naming: the plant has two names, 'Old Man' and 'Lad's Love', though what its bitter scent reminds him of is 'Only an avenue, dark, nameless, without end'. Thomas learnt much from Frost's example (and encouragement), and reading them together is instructive.

W.H. Auden (1907-74), *Selected Poems*. You might turn first to 'Musée des Beaux Arts', 'Fleet Visit', 'A Walk After Dark', 'A Shilling Life', 'Sigmund Freud', 'Oxford', 'In Praise of Limestone' and 'Lay your sleeping head my love'. Together with his friend and contemporary, **Louis MacNeice** (1907-63), Auden has – like Frost and Thomas – the virtue of accessibility with extreme technical poise. 'The Hebrides', 'Bagpipe Music', 'Snow', 'Sunday Morning' are starting points for a love affair with the work of MacNeice.

More controversial but equally decisive figures are **T.S. Eliot** (1888-1965) and **Ezra Pound** (1885-1972). When people talk of modern poets being difficult, they are often thinking of these two. Ezra Pound's *Cantos* are, as Basil Bunting said, like the Alps: you will have to go a long way round to avoid them. But I don't advise the assault until you are sure of your equipment. With so many commentaries available, Eliot's *Waste Land* – it's also relatively short – is less of a perilous expedition. 'The Love Song of J. Alfred Prufrock' still seems to me his strongest poem, though the *Four Quartets* are generally considered his masterpiece. You have to read Eliot; and his essays too, incidentally, which are not forbidding, as people sometimes think (in fact quite the opposite). 'The Music of Poetry' is a good starting place, in the *Selected Prose* or *On Poetry and Poets*.

At some stage you will want to acquaint yourself with **Hart Crane**, **Wallace Stevens**, **William Carlos Williams**, and others you might first look at in *The Faber Book of Modern Verse*, who include many of the following:

Basil Bunting (1900-85). One of Bunting's 'Odes' is also quoted on page 34 of this book. His (short) *Collected Poems* is essential reading.

Elizabeth Bishop (1911-79). Her oeuvre is considerably larger, but she reads fast (whereas it is impossible to read Bunting quickly because his work is so richly textured). Bishop is American. Her warmth, keen observation and unshowy intelligence make her one of the most attractive of modern poets. 'The Man-Moth', 'Poem', 'At the Fishhouses', 'The Fish' give you some idea of her gift.

R.S. Thomas (*b.* 1913). You must get his early work, brought together in *Selected Poems 1946-1968*, at any cost, and this will lead you to want to explore more recent collections.

Weldon Kees (1914-55?). Hard to believe that Kees was writing in the 40s and 50s: he anticipates the 80s and 90s in his concerns, his quirkiness and particularly in the flattening of metre (almost to prose rhythms) in given forms such as the sonnet, sestina and villanelle. Practically all of Kees's poems seem to me exciting, though many are clumsy in places too. 'Statement with Rhymes', 'Resort', 'Crime Club', 'Dog', 'Five Villanelles', the 'Robinson' poems.

Robert Lowell (1917-77). American. The greatest living poet until he died, since when his stock has rather fallen. *Life Studies* is still necessary reading, and I like almost all of him. Look at the way he uses basically iambic pentameter but arranged in short units (which appear to be free verse) with only occasional rhyme and half-rhyme. His grandiloquent assonances (the 'Lowellian Swagger') are infectious, but it's a risk you have to take. There is a splendid – in places very funny – live cassette available. Lowell's friend **John Berryman** (1914-72) is a more dangerous exemplar, since his voice, though Hopkinsy, is utterly idiosyncratic. But you must spend some time with his *Selected Poems* to see what you make of him. His *Dream Songs* are a joy, I think. Though his biography is depressing: particularly his (ex-)wife's absorbing portrait of a generation, *Poets in their Youth*. This focuses also among others on **Delmore Schwartz** (1913-66): 'In the Naked Bed in Plato's Cave', 'At this Moment of Time', 'The Heavy Bear that Goes with Me', and especially 'Seurat's Sunday Afternoon along the Seine' from *What Is To Be Given*.

112

Randall Jarrell (1914-65) is also associated with Lowell and Berryman. He is best known for his indispensable criticism – *Poetry and the Age* and *Kipling, Auden & Co* – though his own poems are among the most likeable of their time: 'A Girl in a Library', 'In Galleries', 'Thinking of the Lost World', 'The Trees in Spring' and his Rilke translations (especially 'The Reader').

W.S. Graham (1918-86) 'Johann Joachim Quantz's Five Lessons' (in the *Faber Modern Verse*) is a tremendous poem, I think. You might also turn (in his *Collected Poems)* to 'Malcolm Mooney's Land'.

Edwin Morgan (*b.* 1920). His reasonably-priced *Selected Poems* shows the variety and readability of Morgan's work: e.g. 'Cinquevalli', 'Hyena', 'Instructions to an Actor', 'From the Domain of Arnheim', 'Loch Ness Monster's Song'. Morgan's *Collected* is uneven and diluted, but I like almost all of it, even so. My favourites are mainly gathered in 'The Second Life' and 'Video Box' (wonderful) sections.

Philip Larkin (1922-85) was a consummate craftsman. His rhyme words are always the right word; and his enjambements disguise the rhymes so well that you can get to the end of a poem imagining it to be blank verse. Poems such as 'Church Going', 'Mr Bleaney', 'Toads', 'Here' and to me his strongest piece, 'The Whitsun Weddings'. Cassettes are available.

Stanley Cook (1922-91). Littlewood do his *Selected Poems 1972-86.* Larkinesque but not gloomy and with a Yorkshire commonsense. He is one of the most engaging and accessible poets, and one of those rare people who really has been undervalued, almost to the point of neglect. 'Picture of a Cornfield' is on page 72, and one of Cook's concrete poems appears in the Glossary (➡ *Concrete poetry*).

Elizabeth Jennings (*b.* 1926). Her *Collected* is smaller than many *Selected*s and more readable. She handles form exactly but naturally, and, as Douglas Dunn says, her poetry is outstanding for its 'wisdom hard-earned from grief and religious faith'. Turn first to the poems reprinted from her *Growing Points*.

Charles Tomlinson (*b.* 1927) has never quite been fashionable, though he has often been unfashionable. For me his later books are his best, and among the most sustaining of contemporary poetry. *The Flood* (especially its marvellous title poem) may be the place to start. Though you might also look at such as 'The Emperor's Garden' among many others in *Annunciations* or 'The Stair' in *The Door in the Wall.*

John Ashbery (*b*. 1927). Ashbery's middle-period poems make it clear why some people think him the greatest living poet. He was a member of the so-called 'New York School', which brings to mind also **Frank O'Hara, Kenneth Koch** and **James Schuyler.** (If you like these, you might look at the younger generation Americans such as **Paul Violi** and **Robert Hershon** and our own **Martin Stannard, Geoff Hattersley** and **Mark Ford.**) Ashbery has a paperback *Selected Poems* in which the *Self Portrait in a Convex Mirror* section is the place to start. Generally thought to be opaque, Ashbery is not difficult reading unless you try to understand him. His poems do not make prose sense and are among the most beautiful in the language.

U.A. Fanthorpe (*b*. 1929). Fanthorpe is entertaining and willing to tackle everyday subjects and so is occasionally dismissed as "light". Some of her poems *are* light; but her best work – her recasting of biblical material, for instance – is as durable as anyone's. Her poems have imaginative energy, richness of texture and quiet, undemonstrative authority. My favourites are in the *Standing To* section of her *Selected Poems*; in particular, 'Hang-Gliders in January' and 'Getting It Across'.

Thom Gunn (*b*. 1929). The early poems 'Considering the Snail', 'On the Move', 'Taylor Street', 'Touch', 'The Feel of Hands', and 'My Sad Captains' are good starting points (*Selected Poems*). But I think *Passages of Joy* and the latest book, *Man with Night Sweats* (turn to 'Dejection'), show him at his best. His *Collected Poems* has just been published.

Peter Porter (*b*. 1929). Stylish, brilliant, self-aware, Porter is not always easy reading, though he is generally very readable. His *Selected* is extremely well-edited, and gives you (as the preface says) his 'poetry at its most forthcoming'. I'm not sure what I mean by it but Porter seems to me – like Tomlinson in a different way – very much a 'poet's poet'. 'Soliloquy at Potsdam', 'A Consumer's Report', 'My Late T'ang Phase', the poems from the *Cost of Seriousness* section and 'What I Have Written I have Written' give you an idea of his range.

Adrienne Rich (*b*. 1929). American. There is an early (considered, technically adept, restrained) and a later (incandescent, jagged, politically committed) Rich, both of whom – together with commentaries – are represented in *Adrienne Rich's Poetry and Prose*. Early: 'Living in Sin'; 'The Diamond Cutters'; the short sequence, 'Snapshots of a Daughter-in-Law'; and 'In the Evening'. Later: 'After

114

Twenty Years', 'Diving into the Wreck'. Later still: her 'Twenty-One Love Poems', 'Natural Resources' and (especially) 'Grandmothers'.

Derek Walcott (*b.* 1930). Everyone should read Walcott, in some ways the most exemplary of today's writers, and certainly among the most beguiling. There is a *Collected* (up to 1984) which includes *Midsummer* and such *Fortunate Traveller* poems as 'The Hotel Normandie Pool', 'Europa' and 'The Season of Phantasmal Peace'; and there is his epic *Omeros* – both of which volumes you will want to get. But I would probably start with his book *The Arkansas Testament* and from it perhaps 'The Light of the World', 'Gros-Ilet' and 'Tomorrow, Tomorrow'.

Ted Hughes (*b.* 1930) is the Poet Laureate. With the exception of *Gaudete*, Hughes's big *Selected Poems* contains everything you should need. Cassettes are also available: until you've heard his voice, you are getting only two-thirds of Hughes. 'The Thought Fox', 'Wind', 'Six Young Men', 'View of a Pig', 'An Otter' and 'Pike' are all early poems. You can't help noticing the patterns of assonance and alliteration, the rhyme and half-rhyme. There is much to learn from Hughes in a general way, though his manner would swallow most new poets' voices. The *Moortown* poems, composed at speed like journal entries, are breathtaking. The long poem *Gaudete* gives no time breathe. Hughes's *Crow* poems and much of his ambitious later work make equally exhilarating reading, but his more extreme effects may seem bullying in other hands and a little obvious.

Roy Fisher (*b.* 1930) is difficult until you feel comfortable with the way he works. The sequences *City* and *Wonders and Obligations* make demanding but exciting reading. I like Fisher best when he focuses on real, particular detail in urban landscapes and makes them his own. At these times, I agree with John Ash who feels that Fisher should be as well-known and widely read in Britain as Heaney and Hughes.

I think this is true too of **Tomas Tranströmer** (*b.* 1931), even though, being Swedish, his work comes to us in translation. (Hats off to Robin Fulton!) Tranströmer's world may seem a little bizarre at first, but – as with Les Murray (below) – part of its greatness comes from a generous, clear-eyed, taking-nothing-for-granted view of the world. 'Nocturne' is quoted on page 62, and taken from Tranströmer's *Collected Poems*.

Sylvia Plath (1932-63), arguably the most gifted poet of our age. Her mannerisms are dangerously easy to adopt. But the fluency and depth of her imagination were hard won and will not bear imitation. The less daring and more conventionally crafted work –

'Mirror', 'Blackberrying', 'Morning Song', 'Tulips', 'Parliament Hill Fields', 'Insomniac' for instance – are models of their kind. You must read them. It makes sense to get the *Collected Poems*, which is still reasonably priced and has key notes and variants.

Anne Stevenson (*b.* 1933). Born in England of American parents, and educated in America, but living mainly in Britain, Stevenson has managed to find a personal style which embraces the lyrical, dramatic and meditative. She described her earlier self as 'a poet in the plight of Sylvia Plath (married, divorced with small children) who wanted to write poems like Elizabeth Bishop.' Her best work seems to me to be in *The Fiction Makers*, which is represented in her 1987 *Selected Poems*.

Brendan Kennelly (*b.* 1936). His prolific and profligate genius is starting to be recognised in Britain as well as his native Ireland. From his Selected Poems *A Time for Voices* you might turn first to 'The Visitor' and 'Yes'.

Tony Harrison (*b.* 1937) has a tremendous following, both popularly and in academic circles. His 'Book Ends' is quoted on page 95. If that's not enough to convince you, turn to the Carcanet or Penguin *Contemporary Poets* anthologies or to the *Poetry with an Edge* anthology (where the whole of *A Cold Coming* appears). He has a *Selected Poems* and more recently *The Gaze of the Gorgon*.

Les Murray (*b.* 1938). Big in every way, sprawling, prodigal with his talent, Murray is also a poet of exactness and the most delicate focus. Look at 'Poetry and Religion', 'Driving Through Sawmill Towns', 'Evening Alone at Bunyah', 'The Burning Truck', 'The Sleepout', 'The Mitchells' and 'The Quality of Sprawl'. There is a paperback *Collected Poems* up to but not including *Dog Fox Field* ('Cows on Killing Day', 'The Emerald Dove') and *Translations from the Natural World*.

Ken Smith (*b.* 1938). 'He writes to people, not for them,' Martin Booth has said. Smith's poems move fast, as if written on the run; they are hard-edged, urban and no-nonsense but always lyrically charged and willing to take chances. He has many books including a big early selected, *The Poet Reclining* and most recently *The heart, the border*, from which you might turn first to the two 'Intercepted Letters' and 'The Pornographer', and *Tender to the Queen of Spain*.

C.K. Williams (*b.* 1936). *Flesh and Blood* is the book to start with. If you hanker after long lines, and writing sequences of poems like interconnected but not quite plotted short-stories, look no further.

Seamus Heaney (*b.* 1939) is another greatest living poet but none-theless you must read him. Poems such as 'Death of a Naturalist', 'Churning Day', 'The Early Purges', 'The Forge', 'Mid-Term Break' from his first books will lead you to want to read his later, more complex but still lucidly expressed poems, from *North* on. He has a big new *Selected Poems*, and a cassette can still probably be come by in your library. But then again, you might begin with the first half of his 1992 volume, *Seeing Things*, which is approachable and achieved.

Michael Longley (*b.* 1939) and **Derek Mahon** (*b.* 1941) have between them written two of the most considerable poems of our time – Longley's recent short sequence 'Ghetto' is available only in the collection *Gorse Fires*, though Mahon's 'In A Disused Shed in Co. Wexford' is in several anthologies. They both have *Selected Poems* in print. Mahon's villanelle, 'Antarctica', is quoted by me on page 98.

Douglas Dunn (*b.* 1942) has learned from Larkin, among others, and his first – and extremely entertaining – book, *Terry Street* is set in Hull where Larkin worked and Dunn then lived. If you start at 'A Removal From Terry Street', and 'Women in Rollers' you will know pretty quickly if you like that book's tone and procedures. His *Love Or Nothing* seems to me splendid, and *Elegies* has won acclaim. His *Selected Poems* carries work from all of these volumes. Turn to such as 'I am a Cameraman' and 'The Friendship of Young Poets'.

*

My cut-off date for that list was *born before* 1940, but Mahon and Dunn got in there anyway. What about poets born after that? Usually, when asked which contemporary poets to try, I go first for: Carol Ann Duffy ('Warming Her Pearls' is quoted on page 47); John Ash ('Smoke', page 55); Simon Armitage ('Gone', page 8; 'November', page 44); Deborah Randall ('Ballygrand Widow', page 12); David Constantine (two sonnets, page 97); Ian McMillan ('The Meaning of Life', page 42); and Sujata Bhatt. Again, there are lit-erally dozens I might equally have chosen. Browse through anth-ologies, magazines, bookshops and your library. Trust your instincts (not the blurb!).

You may have noticed there is only one translated poet here, Tomas Tranströmer. Anthologies are again the starting place (see Hyland). I think you have to acquaint yourself with writers such as Pablo Neruda, Octavio Paz, Zbigniew Herbert, Miroslav Holub and Czeslaw Milosz. Also Rainer Maria Rilke (1875-1926), the great

German-language poet, whose work – in the Stephen Mitchell translation (Picador) – opens up another imaginative world. You might turn specifically to 'Washing the Corpse', 'The Swan', 'The Panther' and 'Orpheus, Eurydice, Hermes'. Hans Magnus Enzensberger's tour-de-force *The Sinking of the Titanic* (published 1980) was translated from the German by the poet himself. And while I'm at it, and finally, Oliver Bernard's Apollinaire *Selected Poems* and Alistair Elliot's Verlaine *Men/Women* seem to me amazing books.

Well, the list could go on and on. There are many exciting new poets (some of whom I've quoted in the course of this book, and whose details therefore appear in the Bibliography). Don't stint yourself. Enjoy!

WHERE TO GO FROM HERE

Glossary

Accent: The emphasis or stress placed on a syllable in a line of poetry (➡ *Foot*, below).

Alexandrine: A line of six (usually iambic) feet.

Allegory: (Greek: 'speaking otherwise') Where a thing or things in a poem – or any work of art – represent something else, *systematically*. The detail or action works on a literal level, but has another meaning also. Few contemporary poems are clearly allegorical.

Alliteration: Repetition of consonants, especially the first but also internal consonants in neighbouring words. We use it to make or suggest connections in a line or passage, or to reinforce meaning, or else to imitate a characteristic of the thing it is describing – e.g. the S sounds in a line about a 'hissing snake'. Alliteration is more than most devices open to misuse; either inappropriate to its context or simply too obvious.

Alternate rhyme: *abab*. (➡ *Rhyme scheme*.)

Amphibrach: A three-syllable foot consisting of a middle stressed syllable with unstressed syllables on either side, e.g. 'arrangement'.

Anapaest: A foot consisting of two unstressed and one stressed syllable, as in 'interrupt'.

Antonym: A word of opposite meaning to another: ugly/beautiful.

Ars est celare artem: Latin: Art is to conceal art.

Assonance: (Latin: 'to sound to') Repetition of identical (or similar) vowel sounds. Helps bind and underline.

Blank verse: Iambic pentameter that does not rhyme.

Cadence: (Latin: 'falling') Generally means rhythm. Strictly rhythm at end of a line, especially final line of a poem.

Caesura: Pause within a line of verse.

Catalectic foot: One with a missing syllable. The first foot of anapaestic lines is often catalectic, as is the final foot of most trochaic lines (except in humorous verse). ➡ *also Hypermetric.*

Conceit: Unexpected comparison between two dissimilar things or ideas.

Closed rhyme: *abba* (➡ *Rhyme scheme*.)

Concrete poetry: Pictures made of letters or/and words, e.g. 'Tree' by Stanley Cook:

Consonance: (Latin: 'harmony') Repetition of similar or identical consonants whose vowels differ. Half-rhyme is consonance of the final consonants e.g. 'lost/cast'.

Curtal sonnet: Sonnet of ten and a half lines.

Dactyl: (Greek: 'finger') A foot consisting of one stressed and two unstressed syllables, e.g. 'happily'.

Diction: Choice or/and use of words.

Dimeter: A line consisting of two feet.

Dramatic monologue: Poem usually set in a specific situation and written as if spoken to someone (but not necessarily anyone in particular). 'Warming Her Pearls' (page 47) is a dramatic monologue.

Duplet (*or* duple foot): Any two-syllable foot.

End-stopped: The line as unit of sense. The *heroic couplet* (➡) is often end-stopped, when it is sometimes called a 'closed couplet'.

Enjambement: Run-on line: i.e. when the sense continues at the end of one line/on to the next. The example under *Epigram* is an enjambed or run-on line. You would not of course find enjambement in an end-stopped line.

Envoi: Also spelt *Envoy*. Concluding stanza of Rime Royal, Sestina etc. Latterly sometimes also a poem in its own right, celebrating or commending another poem or book.

Epigram: Short, usually witty statement, often rhymed. Epigrammatic statements can occur as part of longer pieces; e.g. from Pope's 'Essay in Criticism': ''Tis with our judgements as our watches, none/ Go just alike, yet each believes his own'.

Epigraph: A quotation placed at beginning of book or poem.

Eye rhyme: A rhyme which doesn't rhyme fully, but looks on the page as if it might.

Feminine rhyme: Rhyme of a stressed followed by an unstressed syllable. A feminine eye rhyme is 'over/lover'.

Fixed, given *or* traditional form: e.g. sonnet, villanelle.

Foot: A foot is a unit in a line of metrical verse. An iambic foot is an unstressed followed by an accented (or stressed) syllable – e.g. 'The cur' is the first foot in 'The cur|few tolls|the knell| of pass|ing day...' (Gray).

Found poem: Plagiarism as art. Can be like 'sampling' in pop music; though it tends to re-line prose as poetry (rather than 'borrowing' from other poems).

Free verse: 'No such thing to the man who wants to do a good job' (Eliot). Any non-metrical poetry.

Genre: A literary type, e.g. 'Novel'; 'Tragedy'; 'Satire'; 'Epic'.

Heroic couplet: Rhymed pairs of five iambic feet, e.g. 'A perfect judge will read each work of Wit / With the same spirit that its author writ' (Pope).

Hexameter: A line consisting of six feet.

Hyperbole: Exaggeration.

Hypermetric: When a measure has an extra foot or part of a foot. A foot with an extra syllable (usually at end of line) is called an hypermetric foot. (➡ *Catalectic*.)

Iamb: A foot consisting of unstressed and stressed syllables. e.g. 'beneath'.

Imagery: Figurative language, including *metaphors* and *similes* (➡). An image cluster is a group of similar images concentrated in a short passage; a controlling image is when a single image dominates a passage or indeed the whole poem.

Irony: Saying one thing and meaning another.

Lexical words: Words carrying independent meaning: nouns, main verbs, adverbs. Distinct from grammatical words (conjunctions etc).

Lineation: The way the lines are set out, where the line-breaks come.

Litotes: Understatement.

Lyric: (Usually) personal statement in a short rhyming or otherwise "musical" poem.

Masculine rhyme: Rhyme on final, stressed syllable.

Measure: Term interchangeable with *Metre*; strictly the unit of metre. (➡ *Foot* and *Metre*.)

Metaphor: Something described in terms of another but without using the words *like* or *as*. So that with a metaphor the compared thing *is* the other (not just *like* it). A mixed metaphor incorporates inappropriate terms from one metaphor inside another, e.g. 'Tongues of flame bit into the wood'; 'The sacred cows have come home to roost'. Dead metaphors are all around us...The *heart* of the matter for instance.

Metonymy: Name of a thing replaced with that of another commonly associated with it, e.g. *Crown* for *Queen*.

Metre: Regular or schematised rhythm.

Monometer: A line consisting of one foot only.

Near- (*or* half-) rhyme: 'Cat/cot'; 'cat/bag'; 'orange/Boris'.

Octave: Stanza of eight lines; opening of an Italian sonnet.

Onomatopeia: A word that means what it sounds like. *Bang!*

Ottava rima: *abababcc* iambic pentameter.

Oxymoron: Self-contradictory phrase.

Paradox: Statement which contradicts common sense or received opinion.

Pentameter: A five-foot line.

Persona: The narrator or speaker of a poem.

Personification: Lending human qualities to abstractions and animate or inanimate objects.

Prose: Any non-poetic written form.

Prosey: Any poetry you don't like.

Prosody: The sum of skills and technqiues of versification.

Pyrrhic: A foot consisting of two unstressed syllables (e.g. 'in a').

Quatrain: Four-line stanza.

Relativism: Using references outside the work to judge the work.

Rhetorical question: When you don't expect a reply.

Rhyme: Duplication of all sounds except the initial one: e.g. 'vowel/trowel'. Rhymes can be internal (within the line) or end-rhyme (at the end of each line). Where the rhymes are not *full*, we have *Half, para-, slant-* or *near-rhyme*. (➡ *Near rhyme*.)

Rhyme scheme: The pattern of rhyme set up in a poem. Usually we letter each line, giving the same letter to lines which rhyme, e.g. in *Rime Royal* below, lines one and three will rhyme with each other, as will lines two, four and five; concluding with a third rhyme in lines six and seven.

Rime royal: *ababbcc*, iambic pentameter.

Run-on line: End-stopped line made interesting. (➡ *Enjambement*.)

Sestet: Six-line stanza. Concluding section of an Italian sonnet.

Simile: Comparison between two things using the words *like* or *as*.

Sonnet: Usually 14 lines of iambic pentameter, generally rhymed.

Spondee: A foot consisting of two stressed syllables, as in 'playwright'.

Stanza: (Italian: 'room'): Alternative word for a verse in a poem.

Stress: Accent or emphasis.

Syllabics: A form that counts/patterns syllables rather than stresses.

Synaesthesia: Imagery which mixes one sense with another – e.g. "sight" with "sound" or "touch" – as in Keats's 'But here there is no light / Save what from heaven is with the breezes blown'.

Synechdoche: Part used to represent whole: e.g. 'the law' for 'police'.

Syntax: The arrangement of words in a sentence; sentence construction or its rules.

Tercet: Three-line stanza.

Terza rima: Tercet stanzas rhyming *aba,bcb,cdc*, etc.

Tetrameter: A line consisting of four feet.

Trimeter: A line consisting of three feet.

Triplet: Sometimes (loosely) same as tercet; sometimes a rhythmic measure of three syllables, e.g. 'company'.

Trochee: foot of one stressed and one unstressed syllable as in 'open'.

Villanelle: *See* 'Some Given Forms', pages 97-99.

Bibliography

& ACKNOWLEDGEMENTS

Gillian Allnutt: poem from *Beginning the Avocado* (Virago, 1987).
Simon Armitage: two poems from *Zoom!* (Bloodaxe, 1989).
John Ash: poem from *The Burnt Pages* (Carcanet, 1991).
John Ashbery: poem from *Selected Poems* (Carcanet, 1986).
Neil Astley: extract from *Darwin Survivor* (Peterloo Poets, 1988).
W.H. Auden: extract from Foreword to *Collected Shorter Poems* (Faber, 1966).
Basil Bunting: poem from *Collected Poems* (Fulcrum, 1970; Oxford, 1978).
Lord Byron: poem and extract from poem from *Collected Poems* (Oxford).
Ciaran Carson: poem from *Belfast Confetti* (Gallery, 1986; Bloodaxe, 1987).
Gillian Clarke: poem from *Selected Poems* (Carcanet, 1985).
Samuel Taylor Coleridge and **William Wordsworth:** *Lyrical Ballads* (1805), from Collins edition (1968).
Samuel Taylor Coleridge: extract from *Biographia Literaria*, chapter XVIII (1817), from Dent edition (1965, 1971).
David Constantine: two poems from *Selected Poems* (Bloodaxe, 1991).
Stanley Cook: poems from *Seeing Your Meaning* (Huddersfield Polytechnic 1985) and *Selected Poems 1972-86* (Littlewood, 1986).
Duncan Curry: poem by permission of the author
Emily Dickinson: poem from *Complete Poems* (Faber, 1970).
Carol Ann Duffy: poems from *Standing Female Nude* (Anvil Press Poetry, 1985) and *Selling Manhattan* (Anvil Press Poetry, 1987).
T.S. Eliot: extracts from *Selected Prose* (Faber, 1975).
Mabel Ferrett: poem from *Humber Bridge* (Littlewood, 1986).
Peter Finch: *How to Publish Your Poetry* (Allison & Busby, revised 1991).
Robert Frost: extract from poem in *Selected Poems* (Penguin, 1973).
Thomas Hardy: poem from *Complete Poems* (Macmillan, 1976).
Tony Harrison: poem from *Selected Poems* (Penguin, 1984).
Geoff Hattersley: poem from *Don't Worry* (Bloodaxe, 1994).
Ted Hughes: two lines from 'Wind' in *Selected Poems* (Faber, 1982).
Paul Hyland: *Getting Into Poetry* (Bloodaxe, 1992).
Randall Jarrell: *Poetry and the Age* (1955; Faber, 1973).
Randall Jarrell: *Kipling, Auden & Co* (Carcanet, 1981).
Samuel Johnson: extract from 'Vanity of Human Wishes', *The Complete English Poems* (Penguin, 1971).
John Keats: extracts from *Selected Letters*, ed. Gittings (Oxford, 1970); poems from *Poetical Works* (Oxford, 1956).
Tom Leonard: poem from *Intimate Voices* (Galloping Dog, 1983).
David Lodge: extract from *Working with Structuralism* (Routledge, 1980).
Roger McGough: extract from poem in *Gig* (Cape, 1970).
Ian McMillan: two poems from *Selected Poems* (Carcanet, 1986).
Derek Mahon: poem from *Selected Poems* (Viking Penguin/Gallery, 1992).
Les Murray: extracts from *The Paperbark Tree* (Carcanet, 1992).
Flannery O'Connor: *Mystery and Manners: Selected Prose* (Faber, 1969).
Evangeline Paterson: poem from *Lucifer at the Fair* (Taxus, 1992).
Ezra Pound: *Literary Essays* (Faber 1954, 1974) and *Selected Prose* (Faber 1973, 1978).
Craig Raine: extract from *Haydn and the Valve Trumpet* (Faber, 1990).

Deborah Randall: poem from *The Sin Eater* (Bloodaxe, 1989).

Adrienne Rich: quoted in *Contemporary Poetry in America* (Longman, 1989).

Christina Rossetti: poem quoted from *The Golden Treasury of Longer Poems* (Everyman 1921, reprinted 1967).

Michael Schmidt: extracts from *Reading Modern Poetry* (Routledge, 1989).

William Stafford: poem from *Stories That Could Be True: New and Collected Poems* (Harper & Row, 1977).

Tomas Tranströmer: poem from *Collected Poems*, translated by Robin Fulton (Bloodaxe, 1987).

John Wain: extract from *Interpretations* (RKP, 1955, reprinted 1969).

Graham Wallace: extract from essay in *Creativity* (Penguin, 1970).

Andrew Waterman: extract from *Out for the Elements* (Carcanet, 1981).

René Wellek and Austin Warren: extract from *Theory of Literature* (1973; Penguin, 1979).

William Carlos Williams: poem from *Collected Poems* (Carcanet, 1987).

Joyce Woodward: poem by permission of the author.

Thomas Wyatt: poem from *Collected Poems* (Liverpool University Press, 1969).

Reference books:

Throughout I've had recourse to reference texts and anthologies. The most useful I've found is Ruth Miller and Robert A. Greenberg's *Poetry: An Introduction* (Macmillan, 1981). Paul Hyland's *Getting Into Poetry* (Bloodaxe, 1992) includes listings of poetry magazines and publishers. Other useful reference publications include:

David Hart: *Poetry Listing* (Wood Wind Publications, 42 All Saints Road, King's Heath, Birmingham B14 7LL: *annual*).

Writers' & Artists Yearbook (A & C Black: *annual*).

Small Presses & Little Magazines of the UK and Ireland (Oriel Bookshop, The Friary, Cardiff CF1 4AA: £2.50 inc p&p).

The Writer's Handbook (Papermac).

Directory of Writers' Circles (from Jill Dick, Oldacre, Horderns Park Road, Chapel-en-le-Frith, Derbyshire SK12 6SY).

Alex Preminger: *Princeton Encyclopedia of Poetry and Poetics* (Princeton).

Some Useful Addresses

ORGANISATIONS

The Poetry Society
22 Betterton Street
Covent Garden
London WC2H 9BU
☎ 071-240 4810   FAX 071-240 4818

The Poetry Book Society
10 Barley Mow Passage
London W4 4PH
☎ 081-994 6477   FAX 081-994 1533

Poetry Ireland
The Austin Clarke Library
44 Upper Mount Street
Dublin 2
Ireland
☎ 01-610320

**The Welsh Academy/
Yr Academi Gymreig**
3rd Floor
Mount Stuart House
Mount Stuart Square
Cardiff CF1 6DQ
☎ 0222-492025

Association of Little Presses
30 Greenhill
Hampstead High Street
London NW3 5UA
☎ 071-435 1889

The Society of Authors
84 Drayton Gardens
London SW10 9SB
☎ 071-373 6642

Arts Councils

Arts Council of Great Britain
14 Great Peter Street
London SW1P 3NQ
☎ 071-333 0100   FAX 071-973 6590

Scottish Arts Council
12 Manor Place
Edinburgh EH3 7DD
☎ 031-226 6051   FAX 031-225 9833

**Welsh Arts Council/
Cyngor Y Celfyddydau**
Museum Place
Cardiff CF1 3NX
☎ 0222-394711   FAX 0222-221447

**The Arts Council/
An Chomhairle Ealaíon**
70 Merrion Square
Dublin 2
Ireland
☎ 01-611840   FAX 01-761302

Arts Council of Northern Ireland
181a Stranmillis Road
Belfast BT9 5DU
☎ 0232-381591

Regional Arts Boards/Associations

Northern Arts Board
9-10 Osborne Terrace
Newcastle upon Tyne NE2 1NZ
☎ 091-281 6334   FAX 091-281 3276
Area covered: Cleveland, Cumbria,
Durham, Northumberland, Tyne &
Wear.

**Yorkshire and Humberside
Arts Board**
21 Bond Street, Dewsbury
West Yorkshire WF13 1AX.
☎ 0924-455555   FAX 0924-466522
Area covered: North, South and West
Yorkshire, Humberside.

Arts Board North West
12 Harter Street
Manchester M1 6HY
☎ 061-228 3062   FAX 061-236 5361
Area covered: Greater Manchester,
High Peak District of Derbyshire,
Lancashire, Cheshire, Merseyside.

West Midlands Arts Board
82 Granville Street
Birmingham B1 2LH
☎ 021-631 3121   FAX 021-643 7239
Area covered: Hereford & Worcester,
West Midlands, Shropshire, Stafford-
shire, Warwickshire.

East Midlands Arts Board
Mountfields House
Forest Road
Loughborough LE11 3HU
☎ 0509-218292 FAX 0509-262214
Area covered: Derbyshire, Notts,
Leicestershire, Northamptonshire.

Eastern Arts Board
Cherry Hinton Hall
Cherry Hinton Road
Cambridge CB1 4DW
☎ 0223-215355 FAX 0223-248075
Area covered: Cambridgeshire, Essex,
Hertfordshire, Norfolk, Suffolk,
Lincolnshire.

London Arts Board
Elme House
133 Long Acre
Covent Garden
London WC2E 9AF
☎ 071-240 1313 FAX 071-240 4580
Area covered: Greater London.

South East Arts Board
10 Mount Ephraim
Tunbridge Wells
Kent TN4 8AS
☎ 0892-515210 FAX 0892-549383
Area covered: Kent, Surrey, East
Sussex.

Southern Arts Board
13 St Clement Street
Winchester
Hampshire SO23 9DQ
☎ 0962-855099 FAX 0962-861186
Area covered: Berkshire, Hampshire,
Isle of Wight, Oxfordshire, West
Sussex, Wiltshire, and Districts of
Bournemouth, Christchurch & Poole.

South West Arts
Bradninch Place
Gandy Street
Exeter
Devon EX4 3LS
☎ 0392-218188 FAX 0392-413554
Area covered: Avon, Cornwall, Devon,
Dorset (except Districts of Bourne-
mouth, Christchurch & Poole),
Gloucestershire, Somerset.

**North Wales Arts Association/
Cymbeithas Gelfyddyau Gogledd
Cymru**
10 Wellfield House
Bangor, Gwynedd LL57 1ER
☎ 0248-353248 FAX 0248-351077
Area covered: Clwyd, Gwynedd and
District of Montgomery in the
County of Powys.

**West Wales Arts/
Celfyddydau Gorllewin Cymru**
3 Red Street
Carmarthen, Dyfed SA31 1QL
☎ 0267-234248 FAX 0267-233084
Area covered: Dyfed, West Glamorgan.

**South East Wales Arts
Association/ Cymdeithas
Gelfyddydau De-Ddwyrain Cymru**
Victoria Street
Cwmbran, Gwent NP44 3YT
☎ 0633-875075 FAX 0633-875389
Area covered: South Glamorgan, Mid
Glamorgan, Gwent, Districts of Radnor
and Brecknock in Powys and Cardiff.

CRITICAL SERVICES

Many Regional Arts organisations offer
excellent critical services free or at a
very reasonable cost. Others include:

Poetry Society Critical Service
22 Betterton Street
Covent Garden
London WC2H 9BU

Poetry Ireland Critical Service
The Austin Clarke Library
44 Upper Mount Street
Dublin 2, Ireland

School of Poets Critical Service
Scottish Poetry Library
Tweeddale Court, 14 High Street
Edinburgh EH1 1TE

Oriel Critical Service
Oriel Bookshop
The Friary
Cardiff CF1 4AA

WRITING COURSES

The Arvon Foundation
Totleigh Barton
Sheepwash
Beaworthy
Devon EX21 5NS
☎ 040923-338

The Arvon Foundation
Lumb Bank
Heptonstall
Hebden Bridge
West Yorkshire HX7 6DF
☎ 0422-843714

The Arvon Foundation
Moniack Mhor
Moniack
Kirkhill
Inverness IV5 7PQ
☎ 0463-83336

Friends of Arvon
c/o Edna Eglinton
9 North Street
North Tawton
Devon EX20 2DE

The Taliesin Trust
Tŷ Newydd
Llanystumdwy
Cricieth
Gwynedd LL52 0LW
☎ 0766-522811

Loch Ryan Writers
Loch Ryan Hotel
119 Sidbury
Worcester WR5 2DH
☎ 0905-351143

The Hen House
(*women's courses*)
North Thoresby
Lincs DN36 5QL

The Poet's House
James Simmons & Janice Fitzpatrick
80 Portmuck Road
Island Magee
Co. Antrim
Northern Ireland
☎ 09603-82646

Fen Farm Writing Courses
10 Angel Hill
Bury St Edmunds
Suffolk IP33 1UZ
☎ 0379-898741 *or* 0284-753110

Old Hall
Margaret Steward & Peter Scupham
South Burlingham
Norwich NR13 4EY
☎ 0493-750804

The Poetry Business
51 Byram Arcade
Huddersfield HD1 1ND
☎ 0484-434840

BLOODAXE POETRY HANDBOOKS: 1

Getting into Poetry
by PAUL HYLAND

This book helps readers, writers and teachers to hack their way into the jungle of contemporary poetry. It informs, demystifies, illuminates and excites. It gives a realistic account of the poetry scene in Britain and Ireland, corrects common misconceptions and allows young or new writers to see themselves in context. Paul Hyland has written the book he wanted to read when he started getting into poetry.

- **Modernists to Martians:** Groups, movements, fashions and influences. Jargon and hype: what it all means in plain English, from the ludic to the ludicrous.

- **Key books:** Which are the most important collections and the most influential anthologies? Which are the poems of our time?

- **Poetry readings:** The circuit and the circus. The importance of the ear, the power of the spoken word *versus* the ego-trip turn-off.

- **Getting into print:** The editor's eye view. Submitting to magazines and publishers. How to target editors and save time, paper and money.

- **Competitions and prizes:** Winning words. Competition poems. Do prizes lead to publication? Awards and bursaries.

- **Organisations:** Poetry societies, Arts Councils, regional arts boards. Who your allies are. How they help and how you should approach them.

- **Critical help:** Where you can get feedback and advice. Postal services, pundits and gurus. Courses, workshops and writers-in-residence.

- **Nice Little Earners:** Jobs poets can do. Readings, schools, residencies.

- **Resources:** A wealth of information and listings, together with provocative chapters on both Riches and Paranoia.

Paul Hyland is a full-time freelance writer. He won an Eric Gregory Award in 1976 and the Alice Hunt Bartlett Award in 1985. He is an experienced reader and teacher. He has published three travel/topographical books, including *The Black Heart: A Voyage into Central Africa* (Gollancz, 1988). Bloodaxe produced his *Poems of Z* (1982) and *The Stubborn Forest* (1984), and will publish his next collection. His work has appeared in many magazines and anthologies, and his poetry, plays and features have been broadcast on BBC Radio 3 & 4.

Paperback £6.95   **112 pages**   **ISBN 1 85224 118 7**